'Identical twins are and have often be
notably, with the heritability of inte
tural preoccupations. In this book, Ncube critiques these twin traditions and
sets them aside, in order to listen to the accounts given by identical twins
themselves. This book provides a unique perspective, founded in the views
on township of twins themselves.'

Professor Corinne Squire, *Co-Director, Centre for Narrative Research,*
School of Social Sciences, University of East London, UK

'In this illuminating book, Dr Ncube provides an account of twin identities
that is a refreshing change from much of the related psychological studies
on twins. He steps out with mainstream psychology by incorporating elements of social constructionism and poststructuralism to offer an account of
twin identities that is less concerned with the internal psyche than with the
external forces and representation influences on the production of the cat-
egory of twins.'

Dr Ken McLaughlin, *Senior Lecturer, Manchester*
Metropolitan University, UK

'This is a very important contribution to the fields of cultural studies, iden-.
tity and social psychology. The author's engagement of cultural and first
person accounts in an attempt to understand identities, their performance
and the emerging social narratives as products of social construction makes
it rich. Discourses on representation; its impact on the construction of, and
creation of 'narrativised' performative sequences of identity in the structural representation of society are even more engaging. As a study on social
psychology, the book also discusses a very important concept of the subject
position by focusing on how twins find themselves assuming different roles
and performative identities in society; most of which are products of social
construction and continuously represented through structural mind maps
of belonging and narratives. Further, as an important contribution to the
field, the author challenges us to critically understand identity formation as a
structured sequential narrative, which begins with the birth of an individual,
who becomes the socially constructed 'other' and is offered a subject position
to which boundaries of belonging also emerge.'

Dr Brilliant Sigabade Mhlanga, *School of Humanities,*
University of Hertfordshire, UK

IDENTICAL TWINS

In *Identical Twins: The Social Construction and Performance of Identity in Culture and Society*, Ncube conceptualises twin identity as a multi-layered dynamic that changes through performance, and explores twin identity through a social constructionist approach.

Until now, mainstream twin studies have mostly sought to explain social phenomena about twins from 'inside' the person, providing their explanations in terms of internal entities such as personality structures with an obvious underlying essentialist assumption. By examining the theories of Michel Foucault and Judith Butler, Ncube shows that the 'identity' of twins is managed in both an academic and cultural context, and in relation to specific audiences.

Relocating the explanations that we gather in social research, including in qualitative research in psychology, the book focuses its enquiry on the social practices and interactions that people engage in with each other, not delving 'inside' the person. Using real-world twin accounts, the book maps out the social construction of twin identity, and allows for the twins' own voices to be examined in relation to twin experiences.

Also addressing aspects of being misunderstood, as well as the idea of misunderstanding oneself, this book is fascinating reading for students and researchers in critical and cultural psychology, and anyone interested in twin studies.

Dr Mvikeli Ncube is a Visiting Teaching Fellow at Manchester Metropolitan University, UK, in the Faculty of Health, Psychology and Social Care. He is also an associate researcher with Caribbean African Health Network based in the same University. Ncube has published articles on Cultural Psychology and Social Identity.

Concepts for Critical Psychology: Disciplinary Boundaries Re-thought
Series editor: Ian Parker

Developments inside psychology that question the history of the discipline and the way it functions in society have led many psychologists to look outside the discipline for new ideas. This series draws on cutting edge critiques from just outside psychology in order to complement and question critical arguments emerging inside. The authors provide new perspectives on subjectivity from disciplinary debates and cultural phenomena adjacent to traditional studies of the individual.

The books in the series are useful for advanced level undergraduate and postgraduate students, researchers and lecturers in psychology and other related disciplines such as cultural studies, geography, literary theory, philosophy, psychotherapy, social work and sociology.

Most recently Published Titles:

Deleuze and Psychology
Philosophical Provocations to Psychological Practices
Maria Nichterlein & John R. Morss

Rethinking Education through Critical Psychology
Cooperative schools, social justice and voice
Gail Davidge

Developing Minds
Psychology, neoliberalism and power
Elise Klein

Marxism and Psychoanalysis
In or against Psychology?
David Pavón-Cuéllar

Beyond Care
Boundaries to Science, Health and Subjectivity in Capitalism
Owen Dempsey

IDENTICAL TWINS

The Social Construction and Performance of Identity in Culture and Society

Mvikeli Ncube

LONDON AND NEW YORK

First published 2018
by Routledge
2 Park Square, Milton Park, Abingdon, Oxon OX14 4RN

and by Routledge
711 Third Avenue, New York, NY 10017

Routledge is an imprint of the Taylor & Francis Group, an informa business

British Library Cataloguing-in-Publication Data
A catalogue record for this book is available from the British Library

Library of Congress Cataloging-in-Publication Data
A catalog record for this book has been requested

ISBN: 978-0-815-35352-2 (hbk)
ISBN: 978-0-815-35355-3 (pbk)
ISBN: 978-1-351-13614-3 (ebk)

Typeset in Bembo
by Out of House Publishing

CONTENTS

FOREWORD

This book goes to the heart of psychology, taking up one of the key motifs in psychological research that has developed in Europe and then around the world in the last century and a half. Twins exemplify how the discipline of psychology treats its objects of research. Psychology treats the twins it studies as objects rather than subjects, and most 'twin research' turns out not really to be about the lives and experience of being a twin at all. Rather, the twins are used as little living laboratory specimens, convenient for the psychologist who is able to pretend that, because each twin in a pair supposedly lives the same life, so the 'nurture' bit of the equation can be bracketed off in order to leave behind the 'nature' of the psychological being that psychology invariably searches for. One half of a pair of twins thus functions as a 'control' group and the other half as an 'experimental' group. But, as this book makes very clear, the two halves of a pair of twins do not at all live the same lives. Their twin is both the 'same' as them in some respects and an 'other' to them in other respects.

In order to appreciate this complex nature of twin-hood, we need to step back and understand how and why psychology as a discipline has been obsessed with twins as part of its method rather than as the substance of its research reports. Twins pose an enigma to psychology that cannot easily be decoded within the standard experimental frame of the discipline, and this is why Mvikeli Ncube turns to qualitative research to locate twin experience in the context of history and culture. He explores the way in which representations of twins in literature and films frame our understanding of twins and the understanding that twins have of themselves, how discourse pertaining to twin-hood is liable at every twist and turn of the narrative to fall into the trap of 'understanding' twins within the frame of commonsense, a commonsense understanding that psychology repeats. No wonder twins often feel misunderstood.

The enigma of being a twin is enclosed in a series of discourses that include the phenomenon of coupledom. To treat a pair of twins as a couple seems to resolve the paradox that, on the one hand, twins are divided from each other – they are not the single self-same individual distributed into two separate bodies – and, on the other, they do often share to a significant extent their particular life history. Twins thus stand just at the edge of the 'rational unitary subject' so beloved of mainstream laboratory-experimental psychology. They are not completely separate from each other, two unitary subjects, and neither do they function together as one unitary subject. This book thus unravels what it really might mean to live as *Identical Twins*, and so this is a study of *The Social Construction and Performance of Identity in Culture and Psychology* that itself stands at the edge of psychological research, throwing light on that mainstream research from the standpoint of critical psychology. This is part of psychology and at the edge of it, 'outwith' psychology, as twins themselves are.

Ian Parker
University of Manchester

ACKNOWLEDGEMENTS

I owe huge thanks to Professor Ian Parker for the excellent support and advice that made this project a rewarding success. My deepest appreciation, gratitude and thanks goes also to my lovely wife, Thandiey, and Joanna Ncube; they were a loving support in more ways than one during the time I was engaged with this work. I feel greatly indebted to them.

INTRODUCTION

On Monday 19 May 2014, a widely-read free newspaper in the UK, the *Metro*, carried a headline story about 'yob twins' who were 'both jailed' because police 'failed to tell them apart'. In the newspaper, just below the headline and before the story, was a picture of Ryan Seymour, taken from his Facebook account. Below the picture was a caption that portrayed Ryan Seymour and his brother as 'double trouble'. The story's first line described how twin brothers who were caught on camera taking part in a mass brawl were given the 'same jail sentence' owing to police failure to tell them apart. This sentence and the details of this story offer an important insight into some of the experiences of identical twins and the social construction of their identity – which is the focus of this book. I cite this story to begin my book because it offers insight into almost everything I deal with within it, to varying degrees. It illustrates some interesting questions in terms of twin experiences and the social construction of their identity, which I discuss at length in different chapters. For example, the question of conventional stereotypes of 'twin similarity' is evidenced by repeated collective reference to them as 'twins' not as unique individuals and the similar treatment by the judge who gave them 'similar jail terms' despite the fact that one twin did more than the other in committing the crime.

The following points in the story illustrate important things about the social construction of twin identity. First, the issue of undermining individual uniqueness of twins, imposing of similarity on them and treating them as a unit, which results in the construction of a 'couple' rather than two unique individual identities. It is noteworthy that the journalist chose to construct a joint identity for the headline, referring to Ryan and Grant Seymour as 'twins' despite knowing their full names. That joint identity also introduces a metaphor for couple representation, which I address in detail in Chapter 5, treating the twins as a unit. The phrase 'double trouble' further emphasises the metaphor of a couple, while undermining the brothers as individual subjects, something I deal with extensively in Chapter 3. Throughout the story Ryan and Grant are referred to by their full names only once, while the term 'twins' appears at least three times.

Second, the article speaks to the issue of underlying assumptions about twin similarity. It is very interesting that, although the twin brothers have unique names that do not rhyme (Ryan and Grant), the journalist constructed and imposed the stereotype of 'rhyme' upon them by calling them 'double trouble'. Not only does that term impose similarity on the siblings, it also potentially reinforces notions of pathology, prejudice and stigma in relation to identical twins.

Third, the story illustrates how twin identity can be performed. Ryan and Grant Seymour are described as wearing blue shorts and being stripped to the waist during the time of the attack – as a result of which the police could not prove 'who did what'. From the context of the story it appears they deliberately adopted a confusing identity. I address the issue of 'performance of twin identity' in Chapter 4, including construction of identity around similarity, team work, complimentary halves and identity confusion.

I find the social construction of twin identity problematic in this story because the reporting repeats the limitations of mainstream psychological research, where conventional stereotypes of a supposed 'twin similarity' are reinforced thereby undermining personal uniqueness and authentic individual differences. In addition, notions of twin pathology, prejudice and stigma are also reinforced in the way the story describes twins.

This story makes a significant contribution in setting up this book, especially the arguments I make for using a social constructionist approach in the following chapters because in mainstream psychological studies the 'voices' of twins are missing.

Twins next door

Identical twins seem to be 'natural' subjects of curiosity in Western society. A friend of mine who is an identical twin, who lives in Leeds and who was my neighbour, told me one day how she and her twin sibling were always questioned whenever they went out in public together. She explained that I was not the only one who asked them personal questions about their lives and experiences; rather, they were accustomed to addressing inquiries from strangers regarding their twinship, in the street and other public spaces. My friend told me that the most frequently posed questions were the following: do twins have a special way of communicating with each other; what is it like to be a twin; do you envy others who are 'normal people'; why does one of you wear bracelets and the other not; who is the good and who is the evil twin; what type of twins are you; do twins run in your family; why don't your names rhyme; and is there a way of telling you apart? Our discussion that day of the various ways in which people react to identical twins made me curious about and interested in the subject. It made me think that there must probably be something unusual about identical twins. In fact, that entire conversation went a long way in influencing me to write this book. It left me with more questions than answers. The two key questions that I kept asking myself after that conversation were: does all this mean that identical twins are different from the rest of us who are not twins and what is the background to these questions and the curiosity surrounding identical twins?

By then I was studying for my BSc (honours) in psychology, and I took the opportunity to examine some of the questions we had discussed by conducting a narrative study on identical twins for my dissertation. However, I interviewed only one participant, my friend, and thus my findings did not satisfy either of us; I felt more could be done. I resolved to take the study to a higher level and to extend it to a larger scale, which eventually led to the writing of this book.

Why self-identified identical twins?

Although identical twins usually share similar physical characteristics, only a DNA test can accurately establish their authenticity; indeed, fraternal twins and even siblings can look very similar (Gale, 2006). I am aware that it could be argued that there is no biological evidence to prove that this study's participants were really identical twins and that they should have been DNA tested to ensure such. However, my study was conducted with self-identified identical twins because my interest focused on the social construction of identical twin identity; hence, it was that self-identity as an identical twin that was of most importance in this book.

Significance of twin studies

Despite general, although varied, interest in identical twins throughout the world, and across historical periods, the notion of identical twinship appears to be of particular and specifically psychological interest to many people in Western society. Identical twins play a significant role in a number of academic debates; for example, twin studies have allowed psychologists to investigate the role and value of inherited and environmental factors in personality traits and behaviours. Numerous and substantial findings have been generated from identical twin studies and these have had an impact not only in the discipline of psychology but also medicine and genetics, for example. The study and understanding of traits such as intelligence, aggression, alcoholism, criminality and schizophrenia have all been transformed by 'evidence' gathered from identical twin studies (Gale, 2006).

Psychological twin studies, particularly studies of identical twins, offer a means to distinguish between the effects of tendencies inherent from birth and those resulting from life circumstances. Not only do twin studies facilitate the exploration of inherent and environmental factors, but they also help explore different variations of personality features (*ibid.*). Identical twin studies have further afforded psychologists a means of studying both underlying human behavioural and physical variations (Segal, 2010). Twin studies have also been used in psychology to compare and assess cognitive and psychological functioning. Further, researchers have taken advantage of the similarities in the genetic make-up of identical twins to examine aspects of health as well as behaviour, in order to assess the influence of genes and the environment. Much insight has been generated through twin studies in terms of health issues, including obesity and alcoholism. Psychologists interested in cognitive functions, such as memory, have also benefitted from twin studies, as memory is argued to be influenced by genetic factors (Gale, 2006).

Evolutionary psychologists also use evidence gathered from twin studies to establish genetic determination. Studying twin groups facilitates psychologists' understanding of how the combination of genes and the environment interacts and affects character (*ibid.*). This further allows psychologists to explore the effects of the interaction between nurture and nature regarding other aspects of character such as values, strengths and vulnerabilities (Segal, 1990). Adopted twin studies are also valuable to psychologists, in making room for researchers to assess and determine the influence of natural and genetic factors on development. According to Gale (2006), the value and importance of studying identical twins have been acknowledged by researchers worldwide because results have wide implications for education, social care and health policy.

Even though such twin studies have made a significant contribution to the body of knowledge, a closer critical look at their methods and working terms leaves the credibility of their findings weak and questionable. I expand on this point in Chapter 2.

Identical – monozygotic – twins are produced when one fertilised egg divides into two identical halves following conception. Such twins share a gender and common genetic information; most often they also share a similar physical appearance (Walters, 1989). The word 'twin' is thought to derive from the ancient German word 'twine', which means two together (*ibid.*). The scientific study of twins is called gemellology. Twins can either be fraternal, sharing half of their genetic information, or identical, sharing all their genetic information (*ibid.*).

Deng et al. (2014) suggested that individuals differ from one another in all sorts of ways, including siblings who share the same parents. The biological differences in question are called 'variation' and identical twins are not exceptions when it comes to these differences. According to Deng et al., due to variation, identical twins can have a different propensity for disease and can also be noticeably different from each other in terms of their physical appearance. Deng et al. argue that dynamic and random allelic expression – the way in which different forms of a gene produce variations in a genetically inherited trait – does at times lead to different blends of some traits, even when it comes to identical twins. The randomness of allelic expression is therefore very helpful in accounting for differences between identical twins in areas such as disease (*ibid.*).

According to Martin (2011), there are fewer male than female identical twins in the world because males are more susceptible to death in the uterus. These authors also claim that the birth of identical twins occurs at a rate of about three in every one thousand babies born worldwide. According to the statistics provided on the Twins UK website (www.twinsuk.co.uk), one-third of all twins in the world are identical. The website further notes that Nigeria has the highest rate of birth of identical twins in the world and China the lowest. America, Asia and Latin America all have low multiple birth rates and hence have fewer identical twins.

In 2012, according to government statistics cited on the Twins UK website, identical twins account for one in 250 births in the UK. It is also presently assumed that 33 per cent of twins in the UK are identical and approximately 66 per cent are fraternal. Preedy (2007), writing on the Twins UK website, suggested that, despite the large number of twins in the UK, most schools have no particular policy to address their education, be they identical or fraternal. In the next chapter, I focus on cultural representations of twins.

1
CULTURAL REPRESENTATIONS OF TWINS

This chapter looks at cultural representations of twins because these are connected to the social context within which the social construction of twin identity takes place. The chapter does not treat identities as always existing and producing culture, but culture and social context are treated as changing over time and creating identities. Also, as culture changes over time so too does the experience of being a twin. This point addresses not only the question of why I focus on cultural representations of twins, it also sheds light on why the book goes on to address twin representations through interviews with such people. These interviews are not simply about experience, but about experience as represented and constructed in language. For, as Scott (1991) suggests, in order to understand the repressive mechanisms that shape the experiences of particular social groups, we need to consider the historical and cultural processes that, through language and discourse, help to socially construct those experiences. In the chapter that follows, I start this process by examining the cultural matrix of twin representations within which twins live and build their own representations of themselves and their worlds.

This chapter looks at representations of identical twins in Western society and the way in which their identity is accounted for. In this chapter, I particularly focus on films and books, as they are a rich source of twin representations in Western culture. This chapter, among other things, offers a socio-cultural review of the Western context for those interested in conducting research on twin identity or accounts of twins' lives. This chapter aims to highlight how identical twins are represented in Western popular culture and to critically discuss the implications and significance of such representations of identical twins and of Western society at large. I argue that the representation of twins in popular culture misrepresents them and I question why twins' own voices are missing in those representations.

This chapter seeks to review themes that emerge from a broad range of cultural texts, such as one play and films and books. I draw on thematic analysis, as described by Braun and Clarke (2006), to identify and review the patterns of data. I want to provide a rich thematic review of twin representations so that the reader can gain a clear sense of predominant twin themes in Western popular culture. The review in this chapter does not go beyond what is written in the texts. It focuses solely on how identical twins are represented in the films, books and play. I then critically discuss the significance, implications and meanings of those representations of identical twins and Western society at large in light of other studies too.

Culture, according to Griffin (2000, p. 17), can be seen 'as traditional and communicated meanings and practices [focusing] on how these meanings and practices are lived individually, how they affect identities and subjectivities'. This chapter briefly outlines the concept of representation and presents some theory of visual and written fictional and cultural representation. I briefly explore both cultural and social representations, as these overlap and affect each other, including through their social effects. I then focus on the representations of identical twins in three different kinds of text (Western films and books and one play), before drawing conclusions about the possible implications of these representations on our understanding of identical twins within Western society. I acknowledge, too, that the cultural representations I focus on are not limited to identical twins but can also be seen as relevant to other close sibling relationships, such as those between brothers and sisters and heterozygotic (non-identical) twins. However, I find that these cultural representations are more prominent and frequent in relation to identical twins. It is also important to note that cultural representations are not the only factors that affect how people understand or react to identical twins; other factors play a role too, such as economic and micro-social factors.

Before I move on to my review, I should make it clear that the Western narratives of twins draw from a common, specific culture. Amongst other examples, African cultural images of twins are very different to those in the West. Although my interviewees did include pairs of twins who were born in non-Western cultures, all interviews were conducted in the UK and all the twins drew from Western culture. This book is therefore predominantly rooted in Western understandings of twins, and concentrates in this chapter on Western popular cultural representations.

'Representation' was defined by Ussher et al. (2000, p. 87) as 'one of the many social processes by which specific orders are ceaselessly constructed, modified, resisted and reinstated ... they articulate and produce meanings as well as represent a world already meaningful'. Stuart Hall (1997, p. 16) postulated that 'representation' refers to 'the production of the meaning of the concepts and language which enables us to refer to either the "real" world of objects, people or events or indeed to imaginary worlds of fictional objects, people and events'. In this account, representation is concerned with the production of meaning through language. According to Hall, without different forms of representation it would be impossible to make meaning of the world we live in. This argument is based on the assertion that meaning depends on the systems of ideas, concepts and images which are then used to stand for or represent the world. The images and concepts give us the ability to refer to things both inside and outside our minds. Representation involves organising, grouping and categorising many concepts and establishing complicated relationships between them. These relationships between things in the real world, real or fictional, as well as events, objects, people and conceptual systems, serve as the mental representations upon which meaning depends (Hall, 1997).

The place of fiction in representation

Gottschall (2012) argues that a message expressed through a fictional account may be more readily received and may meet with less criticism than a non-fictional message that may be based on facts designed to persuade people. He argued that when a message is delivered via a non-fictional vehicle, full of facts, people read it with their intellectual 'shields' up. Yet, if a message is presented in fictional form, people may become so absorbed in the story that they drop their guard, allowing themselves to be emotionally moved and unconsciously influenced. However, Hall (1997, p. 340) asserts that the word 'fiction' suggests separation from real life, leading potentially to a 'dismissal of fiction as harmless entertainment, or worse, time wasting money-spinners driven by the profit driven entertainment industry'. He argues that a circularity exists between what we read in books and watch in films and what occurs in public discourse.

Furthermore, Hall points out that different genres apply to written and visual fiction, emphasising particular representations from different angles, such as comedy, horror, thriller, documentary, soap opera, romance and sitcom. Representations of twins in films and books paint and emphasise particular pictures of them according to genre. This point is important because it makes it possible to analyse cultural representations of identical twins from the perspective of various genres. The different genres employed in written and visual fiction are of great significance to this book, because society and twins themselves draw from these portrayals to a certain degree and form their understanding of identical twins on such a basis. Discourses on identical twins that circulate in society are likely to impact on how identical twins themselves perform their identity, since identity is affected by culture, and some discourses have their origin in visual and written fiction.

According to Rushdie (1992), films and novels have been widely used across different cultures as vehicles to discuss perceptions of the world. Fleishman (1992) makes the point that fictional events we may read about or watch in films take their meaning not in a vacuum but from real communities; they are constructions, created through the use of language and visual symbols, under the influence of specific cultural histories and the present. For instance, fictional characters in films and literature are sometimes drawn in relation to history, cultures and real people, alive or dead, so they may relate to actual experiences too (Chatman, 1990).

Lothe (2000) notes that different story types derive from different cultures and these take various forms within each cultural framework, ranging from myth to song. Chatman (1990) makes the point that films and novels often offer a commentary on real-life issues. Furthermore, according to Lothe (2000), in fiction, be it in the form of film or written literature, we see a reflection of what people have experienced, how people have been formed by these experiences and what has happened in the past. Lothe (p. 8) still notes, though, that 'the relationship between narrative prose literature and narrative film … confirms the point that those narratives which are part of the world around us assume different forms and are expressed in many ways'.

It is crucial to note that identical twins are used in books and films as metaphors for a number of different things, which writers of fiction and creators of films want to put across; at times, these are not really about the experiences of identical twins but are representations of what film and novel writers *think* about identical twins or indeed about other issues.

Hall (1997, p. 83) argues that a documentary film 'is mediated through the perspective of the person making it'; for instance, a person's culture may be a mediating factor. The representations I focus on here are predominantly fictional portrayals of identical twins in films and literature, which may relate, to a certain degree, to the actual experiences of identical twins as well as to the conventions of representation – of fiction in its various guises – and, as Hall suggests, to the perspectives of the makers of the texts.

Cultural and social representations

According to Moscovici (2001), research shows that social representations connect an individual with their society and people make use of them to understand everyday life. They also serve the purpose of facilitating the interaction between members of society, by giving meaning and sense to their world. By definition, social representations are

> a set of concepts, statements and explanations originating in daily life in the course of inter-individual communications. They are the equivalent in our society to myth and belief systems in traditional societies: they might even be said to be contemporary versions of common sense.
>
> *ibid., p. 18*

Discourse is said to be the backbone of social representation (Potter and Billig, 1992). It is further asserted that the process of telling stories (narratives) allows room for social representations to be created. What is or can be told in a narrative is influenced by the context in which it is told; but both the context and the story are not independent of wider social representations. Furthermore, it is assumed that people will always check their position in terms of the boundaries of their cultural standards, to make sure that whatever they tell in their narratives conforms to them (Murray, 2002). These standards have a tendency to be socially dynamic because they are created and recreated over and over again, as social interaction continues in everyday life.

Social representations may start as an individual representation that is carried over to one other individual or individuals through dialogue. As social interaction with other members of society continues, the next individual may complement that initial representation and may echo it to others, thereby spreading it and gradually helping to make it established (Moscovici, 2001). In this way, members of a society create social representations in order to eventually establish a common ground in terms of understanding their world and the objects around them. Established social representations tend to regulate or influence, in different ways, how members of a society conduct themselves. These representations impose themselves on people in subtle ways, so that, without necessarily being conscious of them, they find themselves conforming to them. As a result, social representations are something more than products of human creation. Acting upon a given society, they are also prescriptive and compelling in nature as they spell out how to do what (Murray, 2002).

Echoing these views, Voelklein and Howarth (2005) assert that social representations are used to create a common culture for a society and for different social groups, informing their identity and marking behavioural boundaries. Their creation and validation are collective acts on the part of members of a society, through social interaction and communication; hence, social representations cannot be accredited to any one individual. They are not independent of the cultural context in which they exist nor of existing social practices and their history in a society. Moscovici (2001) suggests that we should be careful to avoid the mistake of assuming that social representations are uniform and that they are shared by everyone in a society. They should be understood just as general tools used by people in a given society to create their world. Thus, social representations serve to outline an order through which individuals in a society orient themselves in their social world. They further perform the role of facilitating communication among community members by making a code available for naming different aspects of and objects in their world. This social code is further used as a social exchange tool for classifying and naming not only their world but their history, from an individual to a community level. Narratives, in this way, are closely linked with social representations, because it is in the course of telling narratives that social representations emerge (Murray, 2002).

Themes from films and books

I have examined a broad sample of films and books and one play from the early sixteenth century to the early twenty-first century, thus over a period of time during which identical twins have consistently been used as main characters or major themes. The sample has deliberately included a very old play to demonstrate the continuity of some very old representations. The films and books and the play considered in this chapter fall within the following genres: thriller, horror, comedy, crime, erotica, romance, political and mystery.

I review the following films: *Dead Ringers* (Cronenberg, 1988); *Deadly Sibling Rivalry* (Culpepper, 2011); *Basket Case* (Henenlotter, 1982); *Basket Case 2* (Henenlotter, 1990); *Lies of the Twins* (Hunter, 1991); *The Parent Trap* (Swift, 1961); and, finally, *The Comedy of Errors* (Branagh, 2013). I also review the television series, *Sister, Sister* (Bass, Gilbert and Shafferman, 1994–1999).

I review the following books: *On the Black Hill* (Chatwin, 1996); *Tweedledum and Tweedledee* (Coppel, 1967); *Gemini* (Tournier, [1975] 1981); *The Solid Mandala* (White, 1966); and *The Kray Brothers: The Image Shattered* (Cabell, 2002).

As well as these films and books, I also review Shakespeare's play, *The Comedy of Errors*. Shakespeare's text is the oldest source in this book, after the Old Testament of the Bible, and I have included it here for three reasons. First, because William Shakespeare has played such an influential role in the development of Western literature; second, as an example of some common themes, which are clearly shown as the play features two sets of identical twins; third, this and other plays by Shakespeare are still performed in theatres today, which makes them current and relevant because of their continuing role in Western culture.

I have specifically chosen these films, books and one play to use as vehicles to explore the theme of twins because of their clarity of delivery and the prominence they afford this theme. I focus specifically on twin themes in films, books and one play rather than in poetry or short stories, for example, because I want to review evident and clear narratives.

The other reason for choosing films, books and one play is that, unlike television programmes and photographs, which are also probably not as rich and extensive in terms of cultural currency, films, books and plays are culturally long-lived. Visual fine art may be long-lived, but it currently lacks cultural reach. Bordwell and Thompson (1997) also argue that novels, plays and films carry a valuable narrative dimension as they feature the most important elements of a narrative: time, space, plot, cause and effect. Looking at the films, books and play cited above, I noticed that the following themes seem to also feature prominently in Western culture: identity confusion; failure to separate; jealousy and possessiveness; intimacy and sameness; rivalry; and complementary halves.

In this book, I do not claim to carry out a systematic analysis of films, plays and books. Rather, I seek to show broadly how identical twins are represented in Western culture. Review of these fictional representations (excluding the factual account of the Kray twins by Craig Cabell) will, alongside my work on social representations, also adopt ideas from the work of Braun and Clarke (2006), particularly on identifying and reviewing patterns of data; this constitutes, however, an indicative heuristic rather than a full thematic analysis. The films, books and play are important because popular culture can potentially validate or invalidate particular representations about identical twins. The validated and invalidated representations may have different effects on identical twins, as some may draw from these to understand themselves. Besides, the ways in which identical twins are represented in films, plays and novels appear to ignore some of their experiences; this will also be seen in some of the films, books and the play that I cite. I now focus on some of the themes found in these texts.

Identity confusion

A tendency to impose certain values and identities, including a misrepresentation of identical twins in films and novels, can be clearly demonstrated in the theme of 'identity confusion' that often appears in the material I analyse. Films and novels that construct and reflect this theme appear to promote the traditional stereotypes that assume that if people are identical twins they should have similar and rhyming names and similar personalities. This representation undermines the individual differences in identical twins. For example, in Shakespeare's *Comedy of Errors* ([1602] 2014), the two sets of identical twins are given the same first names. This not only links their identities but also effectively imposes identity confusion and a sense of 'oneness'. Their individuality is further downplayed by a deliberate avoidance of using their surnames.

The play features two sets of identical twin boys born on the same night to two different women. One mother is very poor and sells her twins to the other woman, who is rich and married to a businessman, so that they can be servants to her twins. Each set of twins is depicted in the play as identical, both physically and in terms of their personality.

Each set shares a similar first name. The names of the rich woman's twin siblings are Antipholus of Ephesus and Antipholus of Syracuse. The set bought from the poor woman are called Dromio of Ephesus and Dromio of Syracuse. Their surnames were not used by the twins in their childhood, to deliberately allow room for confusion.

The film *Lies of the Twins* (Hunter, 1991) breaks away from the cultural stereotype of assumed personality similarities to some extent. Identity confusion is, however, indirectly implied. We see elements of this theme deliberately imposed and promoted through the alliteration in their names, James and Jonathan. The physical similarity of identical twins is represented and pathologised by depicting it as a tool employed by twins for philandering and other immoral habits. Male identical twins, in particular, are represented as people who tend to take advantage of their looks to manipulate women, enjoying the possibilities without remorse. The film also indirectly portrays identical twins as people who have telepathic tendencies; this is despite the fact that studies exploring twin telepathy, for example by Lykken (1982), have consistently found no evidence for it.

Lies of the Twins is a romantic film, featuring as the main figures a set of male identical twin brothers, Jonathan and James McEwen, and a woman called Rachel Marks. Telling the brothers apart is next to impossible; they are literally identical in terms of their physical appearance. Jonathan is passionate about his job and his girlfriend tries but does not manage to keep him off work in order to enjoy some romantic time together. James, however, impersonates his brother, on a number of different occasions, to seduce Rachel. He is adventurous and experimental when it comes to making love. Rachel finds herself facing a dilemma in terms of making a choice between the two men. Before coming to a decision, Rachel meets a woman, Sandra Shearer, who shares her experience of the McEwen brothers. It so happens that ten years earlier, Sandra had found herself in a similar situation. She had dated Jonathan but was later seduced and lured away by James. As a solution to her dilemma, Rachel packs her bags and prepares to leave town. On her way, she passes by James' office. To her surprise, she meets both James and Jonathan there. The three people making up this love triangle are now gathered together. Both twin brothers state, 'I am Jonathan.' Without verbally communicating, both men expect Rachel to point out the actual Jonathan. Rachel stands there totally confused, looking from one twin to the other; she simply cannot tell them apart. The twin brothers appear to lose patience and their tempers rise. They violently push Rachel into a corner and start wrestling with each other. Rachel stands there, like a prize to be collected by the winner. One of the twins, James, ultimately dies in the fight. Rachel comes to the decision that both twin brothers are incapable of loving any other person except themselves. She departs for Europe, where she hopes to find a job (Hunter, 1991).

As in *Lies of the Twins*, the film *Parent Trap* appears not only to construct but also to promote the traditional stereotype that assumes that, if people are identical twins, they should have similar personalities, making them able to swap roles and impersonate each other. This kind of representation of twins appears, once again, to undermine their individual differences. Below I summarise the film.

Identity confusion and its associated consequences are the central themes of this film. The film features a set of female identical twins, separated soon after birth, following their parents' divorce. The parents each take one twin. Later in life, the girls meet at a summer camp. Until this point, the girls were unaware of their twinhood. However, meeting someone looking exactly like them fascinates them and makes the girls feel drawn to each other; they quickly become friends. Eventually, as the title of the film shows, the girls plot to trap their parents and bring them together. They do so by swapping homes, thereby swapping parents, each pretending to be the other. This works for a while; but in the long run the parents realise that they each have the 'wrong' twin. The parents thus arrange to meet in order to swap the girls; the meeting results in their reconciliation and the reunion of the twins too (Swift, 1961).

Showing these twins choosing a rather 'naughty' and deceptive strategy to enable them to each meet the 'other' parent, instead of simply going home and discussing the situation, suggests that their behaviour is the result of their similar appearance – it pathologises twins.

In the play, *The Comedy of Errors* and the films *Lies of the Twins* and *Parent Trap*, the individual identity of twins is ignored. Dual identity is thus imposed, as is identity confusion. Identical twins and members of society, drawing on the above play and films, may struggle to appreciate the uniqueness of each identical twin because these representations undermine this notion.

Failure to separate

Representations of, attachment between and separation of siblings are subjects often addressed in popular culture, and also in psychology, which are intensified when the siblings are twins, as the story of the Papin sisters (Reader and Edwards, 2001) demonstrates. This type of very close relationship, whereby siblings are so bonded to each other that they struggle to be apart, is however not exclusive to identical twins, as most films and novels make it appear.

French siblings Christine and Léa, popularly known as the Papin sisters, were not twins. Their relationship and way of operating, however, reflect many of the themes I describe in relation to twins as portrayed in films and novels. Western film-makers and fiction writers appear to turn a blind eye to close sibling relationship when they do not occur in identical twins.

The Papin sisters both worked as maids in various homes in Le Mans; they preferred to work together and did so whenever they could. They were very reserved, calm, quiet young women, who kept to themselves and seemed to be interested in no one but each other. One night in 1933, their employer returned to his house to discover that the sisters had murdered and mutilated his wife and daughter. When they were put in separate prison cells, Christine could not cope with the separation from her sister. She longed for her and was in a state of acute distress. The testimony given during their trial showed that Christine performed the dominant role and Léa the submissive role in the siblings' relationship. This playing of particular roles provides a context to Chapter 5, in which I discuss the romantic couple as a metaphor for the relationship between identical twins. The dialogue between the Papin sisters when they were allowed to briefly meet during the trial process actually also suggested a sexual element to their relationship.

In the novel, *The Solid Mandala* (White, 1966), identical twins are presented as people who 'breathe the same air', an assumption that simultaneously undermines the uniqueness of identical twins while imposing and promoting a strong sense of sameness on them. They are further portrayed as people who are dissatisfied with their lives as a result of having an identical twin, a representation which seems to pathologise them; obviously, many people are dissatisfied with different aspects of their lives, e.g. with their body weight, and identical twinhood may not be the cause of these characters' lack of contentment. They are further presented as people who *obviously* cannot be happy because they have struggled in their adult lives to become and appear different from their twin. Such a portrayal suggests that there is something wrong with the similarity between identical twins.

Patrick White, author of *The Solid Mandala* (1966) presents identical twins as 'stuck together for life against their will'. The twin brothers, Waldo and Arthur Brown, live together and share a bed until the advanced age of 70. They live on a 'nowhere' street, which mirrors their own lives. They go nowhere and simply circulate within the confines of the closed world of their twinship. They are always together and walk hand in hand, like newlyweds; a pattern of behaviour they follow from early childhood to very old age. As with the Papin sisters, one twin is described as dominant. Arthur is presented as unwise and subordinate to Waldo. Arthur, however, is tender and loving and to him the most important thing is the maintenance of their twinship. He values their twinship and does all he can to preserve the sense of 'oneness and wholeness' that he feels with Waldo. He wants them to be 'one' when relating to others 'outside'.

The film *Dead Ringers* (Cronenberg, 1988) uses identical twins as a metaphor for dependency. They are depicted as functioning fully and competently only as a pair, not as individuals. This implies that identical twins are not complete human beings when alone; they need someone to make them a 'fully functioning whole'. In this film, we see again the superstitious belief in a sense of weird connection – a telepathy of the mind and body – between identical twins when these characters claim that whatever enters one's body enters the other's too. This representation is linked to popular myths and strange beliefs about identical twins, resulting in a distorted perception of them. Uniformity is another metaphor applied to identical twins in this film; for example, they both change and feminise their names – Elliot and Beverly becoming 'Bev' and 'Ely'. Their individuality is thus further demeaned, while their similarity is promoted. Identical twinhood, in this film and in White's novel, *The Solid Mandala* (1966), is portrayed as a confinement, implying that those who are twins spend a lifetime struggling to find an escape route.

Dead Ringers features a set of identical twins, Elliot and Beverly Mantle, who as young boys shared a common interest in medical science. Their personalities are, however, remarkably different. Even so, right from birth, they are strangely connected to each other. Beverly claims to lack an independent nervous system, believing that his functions hand in hand with Elliot's. Elliot is portrayed as being reserved while Beverly seems outgoing, mixing well with people in social contexts and liking women. The reserved twin, Elliot, falls in love with one of their clients (they are gynaecologists) but fails to express his feelings to her. The extrovert twin, Beverly, approaches the woman in the guise of his brother, and tells her that he loves her on his brother's behalf. In the course of the film, the twins step into each other's shoes, covering each other's backs (Cronenberg, 1988).

The films and novel that I cite here lead me to conclude that identical twins are seen in contemporary popular culture as people who are trapped in their twinship, spending most of their adult lives trying to break away from it. This representation suggests that something is wrong with being an identical twin. Once again, identical twins are represented as mutually dependent, incomplete and incompetent individuals, who cannot be whole competent and alone. These representations have the potential to promote a negative view of identical twins in society. People who draw their understanding of identical twins from such representations might view them as 'parasitic' individuals, lacking competence and being unable to function without assistance. In addition, identical twins themselves cannot help but draw from such representations, negatively affecting their confidence and self-esteem.

Jealousy and possessiveness

In the film, *Basket Case* (Henenlotter, 1982), a twin is presented as having strange and unnatural powers, implying again that identical twins are different from everyone else; this representation promotes a particular kind of stigma about identical twins. Again, in this film identical twins are represented as people who are unable to live independently because they are so jealous and possessive of each other. This possessiveness and jealousy paints an exaggerated picture of how things can be between identical twin siblings. The film features twin brothers, born conjoined: Duane and Belial Bradley. Belial is deformed so badly that he looks scary and monstrous. When they are separated, Belial is expected to die but, astonishingly, survives. He becomes a sort of 'parasitic twin', dependent on his brother, who carries him everywhere in a basket. Later in the film, Duane finds in himself a strong desire to separate from his twin and to escape from the 'twin closet'. For the first time, he becomes involved with a woman, Sharon. When Belial finds out about Sharon, he uses his 'super-human' powers to kill her, so that he and his brother can be together again.

The novel *Gemini* (Tournier, [1975] 1981) also begins with a representation of joint identity. It asserts that identical twins live in a world of their own and are very close, rejecting 'otherness'. Similar, to the film *Basket Case*, discussed above, here identical twins are presented as struggling to break away from the trap into which they have been. The themes of jealousy and possessiveness are once again highlighted, and portrayed as character traits that impede their escape. The identical twins, who are the main characters in the novel, Jean and Paul, are so alike that they are referred to collectively as 'Jean-Paul', as if they are a single, indivisible unit. Jean views the sperm cell that resulted in their conception as a 'prison cell'. Tournier portrays that sperm cell as making the twins 'Jean-Paul' more similar than different and maintaining that status. It is this sperm cell that causes the level of unity between them, this biological connection, which precludes 'otherness'. The relationship of the Jean-Paul twins is described by the author as a closed circle, fragile, not flexible, self-sufficient, creating for them a little island of their own. The Jean-Paul twins are able to communicate with each other in a silent language. Jean longs to experience life outside 'the isolated island of their birth', their twinship. In an effort to achieve this, he leaves his twin and travels extensively, with no particular destination in mind. In the words of Tournier (p. 196), Jean is in search of 'otherness and solitude'. While away from his brother, Jean works hard to use each new experience to maximise his differences from his twin. Meanwhile, Paul aims to restore the cell, containing him and his brother, and sets off to follow after him.

The novel *On the Black Hill* (Chatwin, 1982) also focuses on the idea that identical twins are mutually dependent and further portrays them as selfish. Chatwin states too that twins share an identity, which further undermines their personal uniqueness and individual differences. Chatwin adds another fictional representation on the theme of twins, however, which is that twins find forming intimate relationships with others difficult because they are trapped in their twinship. Again, this representation of twins stigmatises them. Indeed, those who draw their understanding of twins from such a representation may be cautious about committing to an intimate relationship with an identical twin. Finally, *On the Black Hill* also portrays twins as being born in a trap, which is difficult if not impossible to break away from. Twins are portrayed as very close, content to have each other, having no need of other people and even as seeing them as a threat to their relationship. Identical twins are once more pathologised.

Although it addresses themes I have already discussed, I include this novel simply to demonstrate the frequent recurrence of such twin representations. *On the Black Hill* features twin brothers who almost cannot be told apart. The twins share almost everything, including, on occasion, their names. They develop a fluent but private dialect, understood only by them. They have problems understanding and using words such as 'mine' and 'yours'. Despite their close resemblance to each other, with time, as they grow up, slight differences emerge. Benjamin loves and is devoted to protecting the twinship, keeping it as it has always been. For example, whenever his brother Lewis mentions a desire for marriage, Benjamin cries. He wants to live with his brother always. This has been his desire since childhood, unchanging. As young adults (age 22), the twins reject 'otherness' and live their lives like old bachelors. They have minimal contact with people in the local village and see outsiders as a threat to their oneness – more so Benjamin than Lewis, however. To ensure people from 'off' are not allowed into their world, the twins decide not to cycle around their community but only to stay within the confines of their farm. Despite their close relationship and the closed world in which they live, jealousy nonetheless makes an appearance. The root of this jealousy is not competition or rivalry, but possessiveness – as was the case with the Papin sisters. Lewis goes to work on a different farm and Benjamin becomes angry because he interprets this act as a 'theft of his soul'. Benjamin tries to kill himself because he cannot tolerate his brother's absence; however, he does not die. When Lewis learns of this suicide attempt he leaves his job and returns to the family farm.

Benjamin's wish to live permanently with his brother makes him undermine Lewis' attempts to form a relationship with a woman. Benjamin does this by creating problems with every girl that Lewis shows an interest in or even proposes to. Unfortunately for Benjamin, Lewis eventually manages to create a relationship with a young woman and loses his virginity. This, for the very first time, leads to a fight between the twins. After this fight, Lewis feels that he deserves punishment for hurting his brother, and thus slashes his wrists. At the end of the novel, the twins reconcile, consolidating their small world and moving on with their lives.

Looking at the way identical twins are represented in the films and novels cited above, the implication is that potential romantic spouses might be correct in having reservations when trying to enter into a serious committed relationship with an identical twin, fearing problems on the part of the other twin, who might not be ready to let go of their sibling or might never be able to do so.

Intimacy and sameness

While the representations of the special bond and the similarity in identical twins can serve as a platform from which to analyse the problem of individual identity, the constant comparisons between twins can also create problems of a different kind. It should be appreciated that everyone needs to be around people who understand them well and identical twins of course share a common history. Such representations not only remind identical twins of what they have but also support and, in a way, encourage them to enjoy the life that they have been born into and grown up within.

The novel *Tweedledum and Tweedledee* (Coppel, 1967) describes the relationship of a set of identical twins as being closer than that of a married couple. The twin brothers ignore the 'outside world' because they live in their own world. Such exaggerated representations of identical twins' closeness and intimacy can make some people feel that there is something mythical or mystical about them. Coppel describes these characters as being born three minutes apart and ultimately, at age 61, dying two minutes apart, from heart attacks, after having lived together their entire lives. This representation of identical twins paints a picture whereby everything about them is identical and that whatever happens to one also happens to the other.

In this novel, James and William Bloomfield are identical twins who are referred to as 'Tweedledum and Tweedledee'. The twins are said to live in a world of their own, fully self-sufficient as a pair, impervious to everyone else. They do not need friends and no one is given the chance to come into their inner circle.

James and William are their parents' only children. Though it is not proven, they are believed to have an incestuous homosexual relationship. This possibility arises as a result of their lifestyle, which is closely identified with what Coppel calls 'gay stereotypes'. It is difficult to tell them apart and the fact that they keep their documents, such as birth certificates, together increases the possibility for identity confusion. .

This novel can be seen as a frame of reference for understanding identical twins, creating the impression that they are not sociable because they have no need of friendship with anybody else. Identical twins may find themselves isolated as a result of such representations.

Sibling rivalry

It is important to note that non-twin siblings may also compete for many things, including praise from parents, affection and attention. This may create rivalry between them, showing that these sorts of problem are not exclusive to twins, although Western fictional accounts seem to emphasise *sibling rivalry* most strongly in twins.

The identical twin sisters in the TV film *Deadly Sibling Rivalry* (Culpepper, 2011), Janna and Callie, are bitter rivals. Their fierce competitiveness begins in childhood and continues to grow until they are mature women. Each resorts to foul play and a sense of bad blood exists between them. During a journey after a family meeting, the girls have an intense argument that causes the driver to lose control of the car, which then veers off the road. Janna is badly hurt in the accident and Callie takes advantage of the situation to murder her. Callie then assumes two identities, keeping everyone in the dark about her twin sister's death. No one notices anything for a while.

This way of representing identical twins can potentially promote unhealthy competition between them. Some twins, for example, may be encouraged to point score against their sibling. It also creates the impression that identical twins are able to take advantage of their physical similarity to commit serious crimes and get away with them. This might cause identical twins to be the recipients of negative reactions from society and to be treated with suspicion.

Complementary halves

The television series *Sister, Sister* (Bass, Gilbert and Shafferman, 1994–1999) portrays two identical teenage girls taking advantage of their similar physical appearance to deceive others and achieve their goals. This representation paints, once again, a pathological picture of identical twins and may potentially encourage others to view them with mistrust and suspicion.

These identical twin sisters live their lives as complementary halves. They discover that where one has a weakness the other one has a strength. They maximise this advantage by working together as complementary partners in order to achieve their goals and to overcome their limitations. For example, each twin shines at particular subjects at school and sits those examinations for both of them. In this way, both twins excel. Throughout the film, the twin sisters work together in this way, as a team, and achieve a great deal as a result.

Members of society who draw their understanding of identical twins from this television series are likely to view them as parasitic individuals who cannot cope with life's challenges on their own. Also, it is possible that employers, influenced by this type of representation, might question the authenticity of identical twins' qualifications, potentially leading to a reluctance to hire them.

Above all, identical twins themselves may be encouraged, to some extent, to see themselves as incomplete and incompetent without the support of their twin.

Popular cultural representations of twins: a summation

This chapter presented a review of some cultural representations of identical twins using a selection of texts ranging from the sixteenth to the twenty-first centuries. Other studies might specifically examine changes in cultural representations of twins during different time periods, and the specific ways in which twins are depicted in different genres of film, play and novel, but I have not had the space to do so here. These fictional representations are probably different to those in factual documentaries, where identical twins produce some of the text and speak for themselves.

This review could have been carried out in various ways – for example, highlighting the different ways in which male and female identical twins are represented – but that has not been the focus of this chapter. Unlike empirical psychological research, this chapter did not seek to discover the 'facts' about twins, but only looked at some cultural representations of them as they appear in Western culture. I expect that representations of twins will differ in non-Western cultures, where the verbal tradition is more important and films and novels less so. I also could have presented these fictional representations chronologically, but I wanted to show how these different themes run across different texts.

From my interviews with twins, I have also come to recognise that other forms of cultural knowledge exist, and which twins draw upon, some originating in psychology. In terms of future research, it would be interesting to consider the way in which psychological ideas are an element of cultural representations of twins, and also how older texts, such as those by Shakespeare, feed into contemporary psychological research.

As well as showing how particular themes are so often found in different media, at different times, this chapter has provided a socio-cultural review that can serve as a context for those interested in conducting further research on twin identity or accounts of twins' lives.

This chapter looking at cultural social representations of identical twins helped us to problematise the way mainstream and popular culture portray them. In the following chapters I focus on how twins understand themselves as twins and how they describe their experience of twinhood. An understanding of the socio-cultural background helped me to formulate my interview questions.

Research aims

I now want to briefly reiterate the rationale of my research aims in the light of the literature described in this chapter and the Introduction so the reader can see why they are important. One of the aims of this book is to problematise the way in which mainstream psychological studies and popular culture portray twins and then to present an empirical investigation of twin identity within a social constructionist framework. Chapter 2 highlights problems inherent in the experimental methodology used in mainstream psychological twin studies; in particular, how they focus on specific traits within people and on the occurrence of those traits across large numbers of twin subjects; their underlying essentialist assumptions; and their routine neglect of social factors. These weaknesses can be effectively addressed by applying a social constructionist approach to studying twin identify. This chapter, highlighting themes in the fictional cultural representation of twins, similarly showed up some common images that are not borne out even by the imperfect evidence that exists within psychology, and that again take no account of twins' own representations of themselves. Twins' own accounts are necessary to fully understand the experience of twinhood. Hence this book provides space for identical twins to talk about 'truths' that were possibly silenced as a result of neglecting their voices in mainstream studies. In addition, alternative constructions to those of the hegemonic discourses of mainstream psychological studies and representations in popular culture will be made possible. I now move on to the next chapter, which focuses on the critique of traditional research in psychology.

2
TRADITIONAL PSYCHOLOGICAL RESEARCH ON TWINS

This chapter offers a critique of traditional psychological studies of twins and anticipated key issues. It highlights the limitations of mainstream psychological research, for example in the way in which twins are used as objects to explore other questions rather than consider their own experiences. Assumptions are made about the nature of twins, which are then confirmed in the way studies are carried out and reinforce the conventional stereotyped image of them as individuals locked in a relationship with another individual. This chapter argues that twin research in psychology has invariably treated the subjects of studies as objects and as vehicles to promote social inequalities. Mainstream twin studies reinforce conventional stereotypes of a supposed 'twin similarity', thereby undermining personal uniqueness and authentic individual differences. Findings from these studies imply that this similarity is 'natural' for identical twins and so differences are 'artificial'. The studies make assumptions about heredity, and seem to over-generalise claims based on ostensibly 'separated' twins, though very few of these have actually been studied. In these studies intelligence, personality and happiness are treated as innate givens, predetermined by inheritance, and social factors are routinely neglected or side-lined. The study of 'intelligence' in psychological research has perpetuated a discourse of 'twin inferiority', and thereby possibly reinforced notions of pathology, prejudice and stigma. Twins are represented in the psychological literature on personality and social relationships as having problems with independent activity, as being socially incompetent and as struggling in their relationships with fellow twins positioned as victims or bullies.

In this chapter I use mainstream terms that are more generally used in psychology to describe debates that are controversial and that are not accepted by critical psychologists, for example Parker (2007), or social constructionists, for example Burr (2015). Finally, I critically highlight literature on social and cultural discourses of couples, being misunderstood, theories of identity and performance and social constructions of family relationships and childhood. The specific relevance of each of those aspects will be highlighted where they are used.

Experimental methodology: instrumental use of twins

Psychology as a discipline has been powerful in conceptualising what it is to be a twin but has also possibly constrained, in some ways, how twins are seen and the way in which they perceive themselves. In the course of doing so, some strong, influential discourses have been perpetuated and have been made to appear scientific through being used as working terms by psychologists who take advantage of the power of science that underlies their work. One such discourse, as an example, is that of twin telepathy. This and other related discourses have helped shape the psychology of twinship but have also possibly contributed to the superstition, pathology, prejudice and stigma attributed to twins. Indeed, it could be argued that psychologists do not appear to care about the implications of the discourses they have formulated and attached to twins. It could be argued that psychologists are interested in utilising twins to investigate other issues, in the interests of psychological studies, but not in the interest of the twins themselves; possibly this is the case with other subject groups too. It is important to note that this critique applies to all psychological studies, though I focus here on the representation of twins – particularly the way they are used as 'natural control groups' to address questions that do not concern the lives and experiences of twins. However, in the case of twins, this tendency seems to have led to some specific negative effects. Rose (1985) argued that a scientific discourse consists of a complex set of means to conceptualise objects of attention: naming them, explaining them and theorising about them. That is what appears to have been done by traditional psychological studies. Harré and Secord (1972) have argued that laboratory experimental psychology treats people like objects.

A good example of using twins for the purpose of theorising is provided by Gedda (1961), who, despite not being an expert on pregnancy and birth, theorised that during the gestation period twins are affected by many factors that can cause intellectual problems later in life. The factors cited included: pre-eclampsia, foetal overcrowding, an imbalance in the supply of blood caused by placental transfusion syndrome, and the gestation period itself, which, according to him, is three weeks shorter when compared to that of singletons, consequently causing twins to be born two pounds lighter in weight. In contrast to the above claims, Baxter (2014) identified all of these prenatal risk factors as applying to all pregnancies and all babies and not exclusively to twins. Low birth weight was cited as being associated with 'potential' problems in school performance, which on its own cannot be an accurate measure of the controversial notion of intelligence.

I show below how twins have been utilised, particularly when it comes to the biological or social causation of psychological characteristics; I discuss how they have been treated as objects for experimentation, testing, evaluating and categorising; how they have been reduced to subjects of biology; how they are seen as living evidence for experimentation about heredity; how they have been used to develop technologies of evaluating, assessing and classifying within therapy and reformation; and, finally, how they have been pathologised in the course of being used. Harré and Secord (1972) agree with the above claims. Some respected psychologists actually used twin studies in a way that contributed to social and racial inequalities and perpetuated elitist political philosophies and scientific racism. Indeed, some committed academic fraud to further their own political agendas.

Some of the key research in intelligence studies involving twins, for example the work by Cyril Burt, has since been discredited and shown to be false, because the study results were manipulated to make a political argument (Billig, 1978). Joseph (2015) argues that mainstream psychological studies were conducted using unsound methodology and based on questionable underlying assumptions. Twins were used as objects and tools for the advancement of the controversial idea that people in particular social categories have specific and innate types of intelligence, specific personalities and even a particular susceptibility to criminality. This argument was used to make recommendations regarding class, race and educational opportunities and to support inequality of treatment. Joseph further argued that intelligence testing has been used to reinforce the discourse of essential underlying differences between ethnic groups. Twin research has been used to reinforce the idea that differences between people are inherited and that we can identify these differences in individuals in terms of their membership of social categories, such as gender and class, as well as racialised categories, rather than in terms of social relationships. In mainstream psychological studies, twins have been treated not only as objects but also out of context, without accounting for their relationships, and treated as if they were completely separate from each other and could be understood just as individuals. Moreover, the researcher and their motives are always invisible to the reader; yet their visibility would often cast the studies in question in an entirely different light.

The studies advancing such political and social arguments about intelligence appear to have deliberately ruled out consideration of social influences on intelligence, as well as other factors. For example, Billig (2014) referred to the individual beliefs of Hans J. Eysenck and Arthur Jensen, in the late 1960s, that 80 per cent of intelligence is inherited. Parker (2007) pointed out that, 'the problem with most mainstream psychology research is that it either deliberately leaves out things or pretends that scientific inquiry or interpretation is neutral, and, hence, it gives tacit support to those in power' (p. 8). Such studies appear to have taken twins – their relationships and lives – out of context, simply looking at how they inherit their abilities or lack thereof, without considering their familial, educational and cultural experiences. In addition, it appears that most conclusions about intelligence testing in mainstream studies have largely been based on identical twins.

Scientific racism and other iniquities have emerged and grown as a result of some researchers manipulating data from twin studies. For example, Billig (2014) highlighted that Burt (1917), who was suspected of inventing his twin studies, was also an important contributor to the discriminatory Education Act 1944 – following which children of 11 years of age were tested and sent to different types of school according to educational ability – and was also obsessed by notions of 'breeding' and 'national degeneration' (see Jeffereys, 1994). Burt thus used twin studies to make claims in order to reinforce his own personal beliefs.

All this shows how far-reaching the effects of psychological twin studies have been, especially those that have influenced government policy on education as well as on other issues. This is notwithstanding the emotional consequences experienced by those individuals, who, as a result of such controversial studies, were made to lose out on educational opportunities or had to be treated in particular ways – for instance, being labelled as feeble-minded, as social defectives, as moral imbeciles and/or accused of contributing to the nation's degeneration, with little hope of getting help, as medicine and education had nothing to offer them. Degeneracy and delinquency theories, according to Arthur (1997), were developed through heredity twin studies and they also contributed to discrimination, social inequalities, labelling and categorisation. Some people were labelled as morally sick, which was evidenced in their head shape, facial features or voice. There is a possibility that all these controversial ideas contributed to the promotion of rigid thinking, stigma and human suffering. Nadesan (2008) critically explored and demonstrated how the notion of degeneration that dominated nineteenth-century thought on heritability promoted social inequalities, caused human suffering, perpetuated racism and allowed for the labelling and pathology of particular individuals and social groups. She warned that research disciplines that employ these kinds of methodology 'have the potential to reinscribe aspects of the nineteenth-century degeneracy discourses whilst offering private and state authorities new means of exercising power and control over suspect populations' (p. 163).

Twin studies have also been deployed to help understand how human behaviour plays a central role in the maintenance of health and the prevention of disease. In an endeavour to minimise the substantial morbidity and mortality associated with health-related behaviour, twin studies have been adopted to guide the development of strategies that foster self-protective action, reduce behaviours that increase health risk, and facilitate effective adaptation to and coping with illness (especially heritable diseases).

Rose (1985) described how Henderson and Gillespie (1927) used twin studies to suggest that hereditary predisposition in children could be managed and prevented from becoming manifest as a disorder later in life, through training in obedience, proper habits of thought and self-denial. These sorts of suggestions had the potential to promote conformity to a set of rules, deprive individuals of their liberty and discourage independent thinking. The suggestion about adopting 'proper habits of thought' indirectly encouraged the idea that people should accept being controlled and manipulated from childhood onwards; that children's thinking should be shaped and dogmatic thinking instilled.

Problems with experimental methods

Here, I describe studies that conducted research into the nature–nurture issue, intelligence and personality to support the points I made earlier about the experimental use of twins in mainstream psychology.

Piaget's (1926) work was used by Day (1932) to conduct a twin study on intelligence, focusing on the language abilities of identical and fraternal twins. In particular, this study focused on, among other things, the complexity of grammar and egocentric and socialised speech. According to Day, the results of his study demonstrated the remarkable inferiority of both identical and fraternal twins' language skills. While both had limited vocabulary, that of identical twins was even poorer. This research further demonstrated that identical twins used more immature and elementary words in their sentence construction than fraternal twins and non-twin children. In addition, they demonstrated difficulties and limitations in aspects of language used in cognitive operations such as grouping and classifying concepts and abstraction. Moreover, Day reported that, when identical and fraternal twins were compared in terms of their language abilities, identical twins appeared to be inferior, their linguistic difficulties increasing with age rather than decreasing. Similar findings were reported in a study conducted by Davis (1937), which examined and compared the linguistic abilities of identical and fraternal twins. The discourse of 'inferiority' in the results of these studies is a good example of mainstream psychology appearing to pathologise and contribute to the stigmatisation of and prejudice against twins.

Farber (1981) claimed that a study following up previous research investigating the intelligence of twins separated at birth, raised separately and later meeting as adults (Juel-Nielsen, 1980, Kamin, 1974; Newman et al., 1937; Shields, 1962) and found that only three sets were genuinely separated as babies; 118 pairs were not. In this case, and if Farber (1981) was right, it would be reasonable to assume that that the results of these twin studies must have been 'twisted' to address specific political agendas. This is also a good example of how claims based on ostensibly 'separated' twins can be questioned in terms of their credibility.

A study conducted by Lykken et al. (1993) found a remarkable difference in intelligence quotient (IQ) in an older pair of identical twins who had been raised separately. Twin (i) had been raised by an illiterate couple who had both left school at age 13. Twin (ii) had been raised by a couple with an average educational level; he had also been in the army. Lykken et al. argued that the IQ of twin (i), which was found to be 20 points lower than that of twin (ii), was affected by the lack of stimulation in his environment. Lykken et al. suggested that IQ may be easily reduced by lack of stimulation and education but raising it as a result of providing stimulation and education is more difficult. The way in which the results of this study are reported indicates that the researchers assumed that identical twins should have similar IQs. That assumption demeans the individual differences and uniqueness of twins because, while IQ is hereditary, it is also influenced by other factors such as home environment and experience – and to a much greater extent than those who provide biological or interactionist explanations suggest.

Bouchard (1995) argued that no differences in IQ are found between identical twins separated soon after birth, separated later in life and separated and who never meet. To support this argument, Bouchard cited the case of a pair of British identical twins. According to him, these identical twins had strikingly different backgrounds. One was reared in a working-class family, with poorly educated parents; she had a pronounced Cockney accent. The other twin received a private education and was reared by a professor. Their IQs were found to be almost as similar as those of identical twins raised in the same home. Given the fact that Bouchard studied only one set of twins, and the limited number of studies investigating separated twins, it could be argued that Bouchard used twins to make over-generalised claims.

The entire concept of intelligence was questioned by Joseph (2004), who argued that standardised IQ tests, such as the Wechsler Adult Intelligence Scale and the Stanford–Binet Intelligence Scales, do not actually measure innate intelligence. He gave the following reasons for this assertion: IQ tests tend to assess school learning not innate intelligence; these tests measure very limited abilities at the expense of real intelligence; and intelligence is not normally reflected as shown in the bell curve, as psychometrics would present it. Joseph further dismissed intelligence as a 'grand illusion' designed in accordance with an underlying political agenda to sideline and technically oppress Jews, Southern Europeans, black people and other ethnic minorities. While Joseph admitted that genetic factors possibly play a role in intellectual development as some twin studies claim, he nonetheless warned that standardised tests measuring IQ, twin studies and heritability statistics are not the best tools for examining this issue.

Eaves (1972) reported that studies of twins raised separately following adoption indicate that their happiness levels are similar, despite their different environments. Similar views were expressed by Andrews and Withey (1976), who argued that evidence gathered through twin studies suggests that environmental factors do not affect happiness levels because they account for only between 10–15 per cent of happiness. According to Lykken and Tellegen (1996), 'trying to be happier is as futile as trying to be taller and therefore counterproductive' (p. 189).

In these studies happiness is ascribed to innate biological factors; they take an essentialist stance that assumes happiness is predetermined by inheritance and thereby sideline the social factors and processes that could be involved in shaping the construct of happiness. For example, Argyle (2009) suggested that the following factors can be sources of joy and happiness: social approval, music, religion, sport, sex, money, social activities, eating, alcohol, drugs and good weather.

Research on personality and relationships provides further evidence of the reinforcement of the conventional stereotypical image of twins as two individuals locked within a relationship. There is also evidence of how mainstream twin studies reinforce the conventional stereotype of a supposed 'twin similarity', thereby undermining personal uniqueness and authentic individual differences. It is important to mention that the notion of personality, like intelligence, has drawn strong criticism from critical psychologists (e.g. Fox and Prilelltensky, 1997). Twin research in this area has been used to reinforce the idea that differences between people are inherited and can be attributed to individuals rather than to social relationships. Such research has often been in support of arguments that imply that people exist in particular social categories with innate characteristics. Burr (2015) argued that mainstream personality studies use words as if they are describing entities within people. She also argued that, when a person is isolated, the words used to describe aspects of their personality – for example, 'shy', 'friendly' or 'caring' – become meaningless because they refer to behaviour in response to other people. She suggested that studies should focus on social interaction and relationships rather than characteristics 'inside' people. Social constructionist approaches view the notion of personality and other psychological properties such as attitudes and motivations as present only in discourse and thus as mere language effects.

Bouchard (1994) reported that identical twins who were raised separately appeared to have more similar personalities than those brought up together. He suggested that identical twins living together might be less similar as a result of trying to 'artificially' separate themselves from each other in order to establish their individuality. He also suggested that when identical twins grow up separately they are not under pressure to distinguish themselves and thus are more likely to let nature take its course – hence, the similarity. By conceptualising identical twins as individuals who have to artificially separate themselves from each other, this study is implying that similarity is 'natural' for identical twins and difference and uniqueness are 'artificial'. This study reinforces and perpetuates the stereotypical image of twins as being locked within their relationship. Paradoxically, it also provides evidence that identical twins do not necessarily have identical personalities.

According to Mittler (1970, p. 99), 'the first important twin study on personality was that of Newman, Freeman and Holzinger (1937)'. Newman et al.'s study focused on temperament by comparing sets of identical twins raised separately. They concluded that identical twins have similar temperaments whether raised together or apart as the result of underlying biological factors (Mittler, 1970). Like others cited in this chapter, this study implies that similarity is natural for identical twins and differences are artificial.

Siemon (1980) suggested that when twins are 'forced' to separate as adults, in order to commit to other close relationships such as marriage, they experience separation anxiety. This anxiety is unavoidable in cases where, from childhood, identical twins have viewed themselves and functioned as complementary parts of a whole. As a reaction to the involuntary and unavoidable need for separation in adulthood, Siemon suggests that identical twins tend to adopt a state of duality to compensate for their lost intimacy. He claims that very close identical twins struggle to compromise their bond when they try to commit to romantic relationships and may indeed deny to themselves how much they miss each other. Despite trying to form very close relationships with their partner or spouse, identical twins may always remain more connected to each other and the act of separation is very hard for them. This study, which theorised without an empirical basis, not only reinforces the conventional stereotype of twins within a closed relationship but also portrays them as having problems with independent activity, as being socially incompetent and as struggling in their relationships.

Joseph and Tabor (1961) conducted a study that involved a number of identical twin pairs. At the end of the study, they asserted that, even though they noticed some differences in the characters of identical twins, one of the many things shared in common by them was that they were not able to fully present themselves as unique individuals. In addition, the twin siblings were found to be more dependent on each other – in some cases 'in love' with one another. They were also striving to separate themselves from one another, but were hindered by a number of strong obstacles within themselves, including their innate need for one another. This study claimed that some factors contribute to the formation of identical twins' close relationship and simultaneouly lead to confusion concerning their identity. These factors include identical physical appearance, an environment that promotes the 'twin' identity rather than sees the children as unique and separate individuals, the mutuality of inter-identity, being a resource for mutual gratification being contemporaries growing up together, and always being at the same level.

This study in its seemingly generalising conclusion neglected the fact that not all twins grow up in an environment that promotes 'twin identity' and not all twin siblings are sources of mutual gratification to each other. In addition, this study can be critiqued for failing to take into account that different factors will apply differently in each individual case and some may possibly not apply at all. Moreover, some aspects of twin relationships appear to be treated as innate givens, predetermined by inheritance.

Lassers and Norden (1978) argued that the individuation process takes a different, unique and problematic course for identical twins. This is so, they state, because twin babies are subjected to high levels of frustration because their mother cannot meet their unique, individual needs; as a result, twins turn to each other for comfort rather than their mother. Lassers and Norden further claim that, when this happens, a strong relationship is formed between identical twins at a very early stage, as they become preoccupied with each other and, as a consequence, the mother can gradually be eliminated from the scene, further deepening the bond and relationship between the twins. The problem with this study is that it makes assumptions on the basis of no empirical evidence and is too one-sided; it neglects to address what might happen if the mother received help and was able to meet the individual needs of each baby. Indeed, mothers with sufficient resources and the support of their partner or spouse and older children can easily meet the needs of each twin. No evidence is given to support the notion that mothers of twins are not able to meet the individual needs of each child, making the claims of this study rather weak.

Having outlined examples of the dominant research method applied in psychological research – experimentation – in order to highlight its weaknesses, it is worth emphasising that twin studies have themselves been adopted historically by the discipline principally as a means of studying the heritability of various psychological qualities such as IQ and personality. This type of psychological research, both in general terms (Harré and Secord, 1972) and specifically related to twins (Joseph, 2015) has received much criticism. Even so, since many of these studies have drawn conclusions about heritability from the observed similarity between identical twins in measures of these different qualities, this methodological approach has perpetuated the notion that twins are similar in all respects. My study is not about heritability; rather, it concerns how supposed individual qualities are socially constructed and, thus, also about the way in which psychological research appears as a resource in the accounts given by twins themselves.

Anticipated key issues

Below I focuse on three topics. First, I look at the literature on couples, because twins are a type of couple and therefore exist in a couple relationship. I am aware that aspects of the literature I review on couples do not exclusively identify with romantic couples; however, I have opted to use romantic couples as a framework based on Kitzinger's (2008) belief that romantic couples are the norm upon which understanding of other types of couple is based. On the same note, Roseneil (2006) suggested that, with the increase in heterosexual cohabitation, other relationships have generally also been depicted in terms that follow the framework of heterosexual cohabiting and married couples. Second, this section considers literature on the theme of being misunderstood. I include this because I feel that twins tend to register a difference between themselves and the rest of the social world, which might be manifest in the way they talk about their relationship with each other. Autobiographies and biographies of twins often indicate that they are different and can thus be stigmatised, and separated and distanced from the rest of the social world to the extent that some people may not understand their relationship. Third, I focus on the social construction of identity and theories of identity and performance because this book deals with the social construction of twin identity and I am persuaded that the research in the area of identity is relevant to the study of twins. I expect literature on the social constructions of family relationships and childhood, which I also include in this section, to be helpful for contextualising the accounts of twins because the questions I ask pertain also to their childhood experiences.

Social discourses and cultural images of couples

Hollway (1989) identified three social and cultural discourses in relation to couples: the male drive, have/hold and permissive discourses. The male drive is a social discourse premised on the assumption that men are driven by biological necessity to seek out heterosexual sex, while women are driven by their biological needs to reproduce. This discourse was criticised by Hollway because it justifies infidelity and even rape on the part of men. It has also been criticised for providing a rationale allowing male judges to give lenient sentences to rapists. The male drive discourse has potentially far-reaching negative effects on romantic couple relationships.

According to Seymour-Smith and Wetherell (2006), couples perform and manage their 'coupleness'. Heterosexual couples who took part in their study on constructions of illness worked hard to present a unified image of mutuality and positivity that implied they had a close and harmonious relationship. The couples jointly constructed the cancer suffered by one member of the couple as a shared event. This joint construction, in which both members of the couple engaged, was a sort of conversational duet involving finishing each other's sentences; using 'we'; deliberately avoiding using 'I'; co-constructing cancer stories; passing of the narrative line from one to the other; developing shared assessments; and talking simultaneously. These behaviours characterised the 'coupleness' of the interviews.

These observations, especially the finishing of each other's sentences, should not be understood only as a characteristic feature of couple performance; very close friends and siblings can also behave in this way but they are not performing 'coupledom'.

Blood and Wolfe (1960) claimed that couples are mutually dependent in many different ways. If the man works for pay and the woman manages the home, that couple is co-dependent in an economic sense. Blood and Wolfe also recognise, however, the patriarchy evident in gender-segregated role division, which privileges men and affords them control over female members of the household. This knowledge is helpful to understanding the power relations that operate in twin relationships, particularly as a couple.

Critics may say that this is another generalised and insensitive assumption because not all couples are dependent on each other in this way; situations differ from couple to couple. Couples can also choose to behave in certain ways because they love each other and not as a result of cultural expectations. It would be inappropriate to afford credit for how couples operate to culture alone, neglecting other potential factors.

According to some psychologists, for example Kalmijn (2001), some couples experience 'attachment insecurity'. This supposedly affects couples who are in very close, mutually-dependent relationships or one member who is dependent on the other and fears separation or abandonment. Such couples and individuals may avoid intimacy to protect themselves. The anxiously attached spouse is perceived as feeling unable and helpless, unable to manage alone and lacking a sense of self sufficiency. They need help from the attachment figure (the other member of the couple) to cope with life. According to Kalmijn, attachment insecurity is always related to feelings of vulnerability, personal weakness and inadequacy.

Kalmijn also identified 'attachment anxiety' among couples, caused by one partner fearing rejection or abandonment by the other partner, the attachment figure. These doubts and fears cause the affected partner to be vigilant for signs of disinterest, betrayal or anything that can potentially harm or weaken the couple relationship. Attachment anxiety also causes the affected partner to question their social value and 'lovability', pushing them to commit desperate acts in order to save the relationship.

According to Miller (1976), studies have often found higher levels of companionship among middle- and upper-class couples. White (1983) too reported that couples are used to spending their leisure time together and over 65 per cent of them always go to the theatre and cinema with each other, visit family together and describe each other as not only lovers but as best friends too.

Kalmijn (2001) stated that the vast majority of couples who took part in his study reported that they tended to do most things together, such as going on holiday, visiting friends and family, sharing daily chores and enjoying leisure time. Wetherell and Dixon (2004) found that many couples engage in shared activities, spend their income jointly, share leisure activities and have many friends in common. They argued that this tends to create a joint lifestyle for couples as well as joint ownership of asserts, which has the effect of strengthening the couple's commitment to each other. According to Hill et al. (1976), people tend to be attracted to, and then to commit to romantic relationships with, those who are similar to themselves in terms of, for example, physical attractiveness, socio-economic background, attitude to life, intelligence and religion. This claim is very helpful in terms of understanding twin relationships because it shows that the foundation of very close relationships is what people share in common. Since identical twins share similarity in a different way, the above assertion should shed light on their relationship to a certain extent.

While similarity can explain why people feel attracted to each other, it should be noted that many other factors can also be influential. For example, a beautiful working-class woman and an ugly rich man may be attracted to each other on the basis of his wealth and social status (on her part) and her beauty (on his part).

Being misunderstood/misunderstanding self

As far as I am aware, there has been no academic research in which twins speak about their relationship in terms of being misunderstood. However, many autobiographies exist suggesting that twins could be misunderstood as a result of how they live their lives. Such autobiographical accounts indicate the following: twins can be isolated; they may have a 'mystic bond' and/or be able to communicate telepathically; they can be difficult; they are 'unique' when compared to everyone else; and they share a lifestyle and can exhibit hostility to the rest of the world. These perceptions offer a reasonable ground to assume that twins can be misunderstood. I cite three examples below, exploring this point further.

I start with Joe and Chet Okonkwo, twins from North London who pictured themselves as somehow different from the rest of the world and lived in a kind of fantasy (Mount, 2007). Joe and Chet positioned themselves as performance artists – their lives were their art, although they did not aspire to join the art establishment. In the 1980s they were the central focus of a large group of young people who felt understood by them. Neither of the twins ever passed any examination or had a full-time job, although everyone around them worked, including their parents. As young men, they said that 'workers look sad and live dreary lives'. In 2007, at age 44, they stated that working 'would have meant we would not be as free as we are to think what we want, read what we want, say what we want. We would never have wanted that.' In fact, Joe and Chet despised working-class people.

These twins dressed identically and idiosyncratically, tended to finish each other's sentences and echoed what each other said. They claimed to have never experienced sex. Although Chet and Joe did not identify themselves as misunderstood, their 'unusual and strange' lifestyle could have led others to misunderstand them.

June and Jennifer Gibbons, popularly known as 'the silent twins', lived distanced and separated from the rest of the world. Their relationship featured a sort of mystic bond (Wallace, 1986). At three years of age they communicated only with each other, using a dialect understood by no one else. Their actions often appeared to mirror each other. Their strange bond and existence in a sort of secret world made others perceive them as difficult children. However, when Jennifer died, June said: 'I am free at last, liberated; at last Jennifer has given up her life for me' (Wikipedia.org, n.d.). They were separated at high school, which caused them to withdraw even further. Owing to their level of attachment and co-dependency, it is reasonable to assume that these twins saw their separation as being misunderstood. In addition, how they lived was clearly difficult to understand for those not 'in their world'.

According to Mo Farah (2013), a British long-distance runner, he 'senses' when something is wrong with his twin brother:

> You instinctively feel what the other person is going through, even if you live thousands of miles apart, like Hassan and me. It's hard to explain to someone who doesn't have a twin, but whenever Hassan is upset, or not feeling well, I'll somehow sense it. The same is true for Hassan. He'll just know when something isn't right with me. Then he'll pick up the phone and call me.

This type of relationship is difficult to understand. I considered the theory of being misunderstood in preparation for conducting twin interviews and came to the conclusion that, generally, the world does not relate easily to them.

Feeling misunderstood by others or misunderstanding oneself appear to be common phenomena, which many individuals have to deal with in their day-to-day life. A communication barrier may exist even between people within the same culture (Condon, 2008) because feeling misunderstood may involve something more than words. Another dimension of being misunderstood concerns conformity to particular traditions and cultural norms. Socially misunderstood individuals may have to deal with stigma and overcome stereotypes, and may be at risk of being neglected and/or abused by those who do not understand them (*ibid.*).

According to Condon, being misunderstood may involve being taken the wrong way, misheard, misjudged, misconstrued, and misinterpreted, resulting in feeling unacknowledged and unvalued. It should be noted that some of the words used by Condon in connection with being misunderstood do not necessarily mean that that is the case. For example, the phrase 'being taken the wrong way' can rightly be associated with being misunderstood but it can also refer to a genuine mistake. In addition, being misjudged does not necessarily mean being misunderstood; it can imply that somebody has been viewed wrongly and nothing more. The *Oxford English Dictionary* (1933, p. 543) defines the word 'misunderstood' thus: 'improperly understood; taken in a wrong sense'. Condon (2008) identified 13 indicators that she claimed were the most common signs of an individual feeling misunderstood or failing to understand themself; these are: expressing annoyance, disinterest, sadness, irritability and confusion; feeling attacked, pressured, devalued, unappreciated, incomplete, insecure, dissatisfaction, discomfort and a sense of failure.

Again, while these indicators can shed some light on the notions of being misunderstood and misunderstanding of the self, they can also be misleading because they can also be indicators of other things. Walker and Avant (2005) identified three major antecedents associated with the feeling of being misunderstood: an unexpected response from the receiver; some form of communication barrier or breakdown; and the presence of a particular issue. Once more, while these can help us understand what might lead to being misunderstood, they can also be misleading; for instance, receiving an unexpected response does not necessarily mean that the other person has misunderstood the speaker; maybe they are simply talking to the wrong person.

According to Jonas-Simpson (2001), feeling misunderstood has its implicit theoretical roots in phenomenology and 'the powerful yearning to feel understood or to understand the self [which] reveals itself everyday' (p. 222). Given that the yearning to feel understood exists in everyday life, Jonas-Simpson further suggests that the potential to feel misunderstood is equally present. Similar opinions have been expressed by Mottet (1999), who argued that people have a basic need to understand themselves and to feel understood by others. However, according to Condon (2008), and following an extensive literature review, the concepts of being misunderstood and misunderstanding lack proper exploration and discussion in the psychological and sociological literature.

Duru et al. (2004) asserted that those individuals who are most misunderstood include prostitutes, the brain damaged, haemophiliacs, adults with attention deficit hyperactivity disorder (ADHD), those with chronic symptoms of sexually transmitted diseases, Parkinson's disease sufferers, those with hidden disabilities, those with chronic fatigue syndrome, refugees and asylum seekers, and, finally, other individuals with complicated issues. Generalising can therefore be misleading. Brady (2004) postulated that psychology and behavioural sciences associate the feeling of being misunderstood with many other issues, such as shared experiences, marital difficulties, substance abuse therapy and counselling, loneliness, interpersonal perceptions, self-disclosure in siblings, a controlling personality, validating anger, eating disorders, bisexuality, phobias, and awareness of professional liability in adolescent psychology. Duru et al. (2004) reported that a study on health-related issues found that a vast number of patients complain of being misunderstood after visiting a physician. Among the reasons given by patients reporting feeling misunderstood were being told that their illness was just in their mind or being offered diagnoses that did not relate to what they were experiencing. Such experiences of feeling misunderstood could generate distrust of health care professionals. In addition, Brady (2004) reported that family members of schizophrenics were found to experience particularly strong feelings of being misunderstood.

According to Condon (2008), the feeling of being misunderstood is related to prostitution, employee retention, social relationships, homosexuality; management issues, self-employment and family time, and business and consumer communication. An article by Skabelund (2005) on management and frontline workers suggests that, more often than not, managers make decisions based on information that those on the front line do not have; as a result, employees can feel misunderstood and may create a situation of 'us and them'. Bear in mind that this study lacks credibility because it made assumptions about 'feelings' without referring to the accounts of participants. 'Accounts of being misunderstood' would have been the best way to report the findings.

According to Brady (2004), one cause of being misunderstood is disharmony of perception. Brady asserted that discordant perceptions are strongly correlated with the experiences of misunderstanding and being misunderstood. Differences in insight and opinion may result in a lack of understanding between two people. Brady further reported that gay men and lesbians, who may be concealing their sexual orientation at work, may feel misunderstood, alienated, pressured and dissatisfied if gender issues are discussed in the workplace.

Although the above claim does indeed shed some light on the issue of being misunderstood, it leaves room for critique; for example, feeling alienated may result from being discriminated against rather than misunderstood. Also, being dissatisfied may suggest many other things, other than being misunderstood. In a work context, as Brady's study (2004) has shown, being dissatisfied may be related to job role, pay or the way things are done.

A study by Walker and Avant (2005) exploring interactions between leaders and members of groups, found that those individuals who felt that they were being misunderstood or discounted included those whose communication of feelings were not valued by the group or leader. On a related note, Gerler (1991) found that adults sometimes discount what adolescents say and this lack of empathy often makes adolescents feel misunderstood and alienated. Condon (2008) suggested that 'the perception of being understood is more volatile than self-esteem, since it is tied primarily and directly to the interpretation of a message' (p. 123).

While interpretation of the message can be connected to being misunderstood, as asserted by Condon (2008), it should be noted that there are potentially many other factors that can contribute to this feeling. For example, physical appearance and manner of dressing can cause one to be understood in a particular way, which may not necessarily be correct.

The other side of being misunderstood concerns the issue of individual differences. The notion of individual differences can be problematic in terms of being misunderstood for identical twins because they do not seem to fully correspond to the concept of individualism that is taken for granted in Western society. In Western countries, particularly the United States, individual difference and personal uniqueness are concepts that have positive connotations in terms of freedom and independence; in others, such as those in East Asia or Africa, conformity has more positive connotations, linked with the notions of connectedness and harmony (Kim and Markus, 1999). In the latter cultures, individual differences are downplayed and less emphasis is placed on the private self, separate from the social context; people are taught and encouraged to maintain their traditions. As a consequence, there tends to be an abiding fear of being different, of being a unique individual, as it is seen as attracting separation, isolation and disconnection from the group, and leads to stigma and various other social consequences. The desire for independence and difference meets stiff resistance; it is seen as something negative (*ibid.*). Members of the group are indirectly forced to sacrifice their personal opinions, attitudes and beliefs and to adopt those of the group, because following cultural norms is seen as crucial. Any attempt to display difference or personal uniqueness, especially if it is in conflict with the interests of the group, is viewed as a disruption to group solidarity and is thus discouraged and suppressed through prevailing discourses and other means (Hsu, 1948). While the above ideas can shed some light on the issue of being misunderstood, they can be equally understood from the angle of oppression.

Cultures that supress individual uniqueness and encourage conformity rather than creativity can best be described as misunderstanding people.

In most Western cultures, people believe that attitudes, feelings and behaviours should be determined by the self, without being controlled by external influences. Conformity is seen as giving in to undesirable pressure, violating the uniqueness of individuals. In Western cultures, groups are sometimes associated with pressure, coercion, regression, irrationality and the power to 'de-individuate', to decrease individuality. Conformity to group norms and traditions is often linked with relinquishing one's autonomy, not being in control and being 'pushed around'. Individuals in Western cultures thus tend to think of themselves as unique, because they view themselves within a context in which being different is considered positive and desirable.

It should be noted that the issue of individual differences and uniqueness registers differently for identical twins. First, this is because they are a couple; second, this is because they look similar and are not really individual in the usual physical way. It therefore follows that the Western notion of individual subjects does not relate in the same way to doubles, and particularly to identical twins. Despite the possibility of preserving the notion of the 'individual' within identical twin couples, there is something about their physical apparent sameness that seems to challenge and trouble concepts of the unique individual. I focus on this issue in Chapter 3.

Social construction of identity

In mainstream psychology, self is a concept that refers to some psychological properties within an individual that are responsible for their actions. The self is taken as what motivates a person as well as directs their conduct. This concept is problematic for social constructionists not only because of its essentialist stance – that is, that things have a set of characteristics which make them what they are, and the task of science and philosophy is thus their discovery and expression – but also because it confines self within the boundaries of an individual (Burr, 2015).

The social constructionist position is that human identity originates not 'inside' the person but around them; that is, from the social realm. In the social realm is a sea of language and other invisible signs that are the medium of humans' existence as social beings.

Social constructionists reject 'personality' as a meaningful way of understanding ourselves. They prefer 'identity' because it is implicitly a social concept and it avoids essentialist connotations of 'personality'. Burr argued that to say there is a wild animal is not to detect some essential feature or nature of the thing you are looking at (p. 33). It only implies a relationship and an encounter with a human being. She argues that the identities that people confer on animals, trees or objects have more to do with their own purposes than the nature of the thing being identified. Identities are therefore socially bestowed and not the essences of people or things. They are constructed out of the discourses culturally available and which people draw from in their conversations with each other. The identity of a person is a product; an interweaving of many various threads that may include social class, age, race, sexual orientation and gender. Discourses on sexuality, according to Burr, prove this point.

Burr also argued that social constructionism replaces the self that is self-contained, presocial and unitary with one that is fragmented, plural, fluid and socially produced, brought about and maintained by social processes not 'things within'. According to her, identities are never stable but in flux and ever shifting. They are constituted and reconstituted across different discursive terrains. She further suggested that all objects of our consciousness, our identities included, are products of language fashioned from discourses. She further postulates that a multitude of discourses are constantly at work in all people, constructing and shaping our identities. She warns, though, that suggesting that identities are socially constructed through discourse is not to imply that identities are accidental. She also claims that everyone is in the process of claiming or resisting the identities made available by different prevailing discourses. It follows, therefore, that people's construction and negotiation of their own identities will be problematic processes.

Two versions of social constructionism exist and differ in the way in which they consider identity. The macro version takes human subjects as secondary to, and products of, the discourses that structure their lives. The macro version is that, once one understands the social structures and discourses that are currently shaping human life there will be nothing further to explain because that is all there is. Burr argued that this perspective is problematic because the task of trying to stand outside the structures that are producing one's identity is an impossible one. The micro version of social constructionism suggests that our sense of self is a product of, and fashioned around, the specific linguistic conventions of our culture, for example the use of the first person in sentence construction. Furthermore, this perspective is premised on the view that human beings experience themselves and the narrative of their lives as a story because they are fundamentally storytellers. According to Burr, the self is a co-production constructed during interaction with others according to the 'rules' of communication or information-sharing in different cultural settings.

For Harré and van Langenhove (1998), self is a function of language. Individuals are located as actors or performers in a moral sphere wherein they seek to construct an identity that is morally justifiable. However, to present a morally justifiable self in a particular social context an individual must necessarily draw from different versions of self. Harré argues that viewing self as an entity is a mistake that originates from our language. He asserts that human beings make a fundamental error in assuming that psychological words like 'me' and 'I' are indexical because they do not imply the existence of the entities 'me' and 'I'. The very existence of the word 'I' fosters the belief that people are autonomous individuals; that each individual is represented by a coherent unified self. In addition, the unified coherent self contains processes and mechanisms, the psychological subject matter, that are responsible for what people do. The words 'I' and 'me' to are not representative of entities but are used by people in their conversation to perform actions in a moral universe.

According to Berger and Luckmann (1991), the period in which a human being develops the ability to interrelate with their environment is when the self is formed. They suggest that the formation of self should be understood in the light of organismic development and the social processes in which the natural and human environments are negotiated through relationships with significant others. They propose that people are born with genetic presuppositions of self, yet the self is experienced later as a subjectively and objectively recognisable identity. Social processes are what produce self in its culturally specific form. They further argue that self cannot be adequately understood outside the social context in which it was shaped. People socially construct who they are through their language, discourses and the cultural resouces available to them within their social context, because it is in the interaction of people that a human environment, with its socio-cultural and psychological elements, is fully created.

The problem with the social constructionist position on the subject of self is that it attacks essentialist psychology yet leaves us with an empty person having no essential psychology. It also affords more agency to discourse than people. If human behaviour and experience were characterised as nothing more than mere manifestations of prevailing discourses that would mean people have no hope of changing their situation, or that of others, through their efforts, intentions or actions.

Theories of identity and performance

In psychology, many different theories are applied to identity. That said, the trait, role and humanistic theories of identity appear to be the most commonly applied in terms of understanding the development of the self and identity, especially in social psychology. These three theories above approach identity differently. However, it is useful to view them not as competing models but as different reference points to draw upon in order to make sense of the notion of identity. It is possible for an individual to use different theories according to time and situation to understand their depictions of themselves. According to Goffman (1968),

> [P]ersonal identity ... has to do with the assumption that the individual can be differentiated from all others and that around this means of differentiation a single continuous record of social facts can be attached, entangled, like candy floss becoming the sticky substance to which other biographical facts can be attached.
>
> *p. 74*

Trait theory explains the self as a personality (Catell, 1966); that is, that a person has countless personality traits, rooted at different levels within themselves, some very deep and others superficial. This theory further claims, according to Cattell, that the traits in question can be a product of child-rearing or constitutionally inherent. Trilling (1974) referred to trait theory as the 'honest soul' because it sees people as not acting out or managing the impression they give to others. Rather, 'they are entirely synonymous with their disposition and identify completely with it' (Potter and Wetherell, 1987, p. 95). Trait theory claims that individuals have one identity, not many. The theory further argues that people are not 'game players' who change identities, but honest; what they portray is consistent with their personality traits (Trilling, 1974).

The problem with trait theory is that it does not appreciate the fact that traits can change over time (Brent, 2000). Furthermore, it treats people as though they are always the same, from situation to situation, which is not the case; people's behaviour can change according to context. Another criticism that can be levelled against trait theory is that it groups people on the basis of personality inventories, making it difficult to fully understand individuals and their personal traits; it thus makes generalisations. In addition, group results are used to make judgements about individuals, causing individual differences to appear bigger than they actually are because they are identified in comparison to others.

Role theory is also applied to identity (Festinger, 1954). A person's identity is thereby determined by the social position they occupy. The disposition of an individual, according to this theory, varies and is socially constructed. As a result of being fixed in particular social positions in a structured society, a person tends to acquire an identity and also forms of expressing that identity that are consistent with the social position they occupy (Potter and Wetherell, 1987). Role theory sees identity as reflecting the social expectations of a specific structured society. One problem with this view is that it treats human behaviour as if it is guided by the rules of conformism and neglects to account for individual differences, even in cultures where conformity is discouraged. Another problem with this perspective is that it makes the implicit assumption that people do what they do as a result of their social context and their role within it; that is, it pretends that other things not human agency inform people's behaviour.

Goffman (1959) argued that, instead of being natural, people are similar to actors in terms of performing their identities. He was thus suggesting that people are like actors on a stage, that their actions are not necessarily expressive of their unique personality but instead are expressive of their social roles; people change identities to suit different roles.

A possible problem with this idea is that it seems to suggest that all behaviour is guided by what we want others to see; that we try to 'con' each other into believing that we are who we present ourselves to be. It also leaves the following question unanswered: if we are all actors ron a stage, to what extent are misleading performances untrue?

Jose (1991) considers the humanistic theory of the self. The essentialist stance of this theory is strongly criticised by social constructionists, however (Burr, 2015). It suggests that a pre-existent self exists, which is genuine, true and unchanging. It also suggests that individuals also have another identity that is not pre-existent, but must be desired and created using the cultural tools found in one's environment (Rogers, 1961). Henriques et al. (1984), however, argued that the self is neither fixed nor given, but is a specific product of historically specified practices of social regulation.

The social constructionist position, according to Burr (2015), rejects the humanistic position. Instead, it views self as a fluid product of language and social interactions that is dependent on social factors such as the presence of others at a particular time and their individual circumstances. Burr (2003) suggested that, 'the constructive force of language in social interaction ensures a fragmented, shifting and temporal identity for all of us' (p. 54).

Butler (1997) described identity as a 'free-floating' entity that has no connection to an 'essence' but is connected, instead, to performance. She argued that identity is culturally cultivated and enforced, a product of social construction, which individuals perform. In addition, she asserted that 'performativity' is not voluntary nor is it a radical individual choice; rather, it is a repetition of the norms associated with the identity under question, and that repetition of norms is oppressive. Butler suggested that identity is constructed through language. Language discourses are used to create particular identity positions for certain people to occupy. She also stated that identity can be created through the process of identification because when people identify us we become what they have identified. Moreover, she also claimed that a clear and comprehensive identity has to be cultivated, regulated and enforced. Violations usually result in negative social consequences. The criticism levelled against social construction's emphasis on language can also be applied to Butler's views.

Social construction of family relationships

Gillies (2003) examined sociological constructions of family and intimate relationships by considering how particular bodies of literature have documented and shaped understandings of social connectedness. Gillies reported that those who write on the subject of family and intimate relationships tend to focus on adult, mostly sexual, relationships and theorise them with regards to individualised negotiated interactions. This is in contrast to earlier models that emphasised responsibilities, obligations and gendered roles within relationships. From a feminist perspective, for example Edwards (2002), these constructions are seen as marginalising relationships between parents and children and turning a blind eye to the gendered nature of childrearing. The exclusive focus on heterosexual couples and wider family relationships as the main source of intimacy was also challenged and strongly critiqued for being narrow and normative. The simplistic understandings of family relationships as an objectively knowable entity have also been increasingly undermined by studies that foreground the complex, contingent lived reality of family to its members (Bernardes, 1997).

According to Gillies (2003), three key themes that are emphasised in family and social relationships are those relating to democratisation and egalitarianism; breakdown and demoralization; and continuity and enduring power relations. Morris (1997) referred to family breakdown as the 'detraditionalisation' of social and family life and suggested that it frees people from the constrained and fixed social roles of the past. In addition, it allows people to form new and satisfying relationships that build on the foundation of mutual fulfilment instead of contractual obligation. Gillies (2003) suggested that contractual notions of family are losing relevance because intimate relationships are being placed at the centre of human life. The increase in separation and divorce is not a decline of family and social relationships but rather an indication of the rise of the 'pure relationship'. People are trying to form new social relationships centred on the democratic values of respect and negotiation (Morris, 1997). Instead of viewing contemporary personal relationships as a breakdown, demoralisation or decline, Morris emphasised transformation and adaptation, arguing that individualism provides greater opportunity and potential for the creation of more mutually satisfying connections. Within a new construction of social roles and identities that are not fixed, Morris argued, individuals are at liberty to generate their own rules to apply to intimate relationships – a move that will open doors for diversity in the way intimate associations are expressed and lived. In a similar vein, Bernardes (1997) suggested that such changes offer greater diversity in and plurality of family lifestyle that democratises personal relationships. According to Gillies (2003), those who oppose traditional family roles and structures argue that, rather than seeing children of divorced parents as victims, family breakdown should be seen as offering greater opportunities for the democratisation of relationships between children and parents. They suggest that parental separation enables children to become more actively involved in family negotiations and decision making. However, others, described by Gillies as traditionalist or conservative thinkers, view the changes in the structure and status of the family and the 'decline' of relationships within it as an indication of a wider moral problem requiring urgent reform. The consequences of family breakdown are viewed as destructive for society and social order. They consider traditional family values and relationships as crucial to social order and the stability of the economy; hence, the cultural shift is seen as a decline, gradual degeneration and loss. On the other hand, those who oppose traditional family life perceive positive gains for personal relationships and emphasise the potential for greater egalitarianism.

The ideological construction of the family has been strongly challenged by feminist analyses through questioning the normative dimensions underpinning notions of roles and functions (see, for example, Millet, 1970; Mitchell, 1971). They argue that socially constructed gendered presuppositions lie at the centre of family relationship and challenge assumptions relating to what are deemed natural and inevitable behaviours and role assignments, redefining them as tools used to maintain power. They reject the notion that family structures are in any way natural, inevitable or necessary, and instead argue that the nuclear family exists as a site for oppression and exploitation of women. They also demonstrate that taken for granted beliefs about roles and responsibilities in a family setting actively deny women opportunities in wider society. Gillies (2003) postulated that the study of family and intimate relationships was revolutionised by key insights from feminist thinkers because the debates they raised shaped a more critical approach to the study of family relationships, adding new theoretical dimensions. For example, Ribbens (1994) demonstrated that the social construction of male and female sexual roles was the tool used to exclude women from the public sphere on the grounds of their reproductive responsibilities, which were confined to the private space of the family. The deconstruction of this public–private dichotomy was a direct result of debates raised by feminists demanding recognition of the power dynamics at work in all spheres of life. They further disputed the implicit notion that family is the site of harmonious, well-adapted social interaction. Foregrounding their analysis on a politics of experience, feminists highlighted how family ideals of domestic privacy and autonomy could hide and facilitate injustice, abuse and cruelty. Studies that highlighted the prevalence of child abuse, rape and domestic violence within the home called into question the previously dominant image of family as a secure, comfortable haven. The highlighting of violence and abuse as common features of family life indicated not only the vulnerability of people within the home environment but also the different ways in which children, women and men might experience family.

Social construction of childhood

According to Aries (1962), childhood is a structural site. Sereceno (2004), too, argues that childhood is not a natural process but a social construction because it is society that determines when one is a child and when one becomes an adult. For example, society places an expectation on a nursery-age child to be able to play with toys, talk and walk. If the child is unable to do so, they are considered to be undeveloped. At 11 years of age, children are expected to be able to read, write and understand simple mathematics. If a child fails to reach these goals, it is assumed that something must be wrong with them. In order to understand the social construction of childhood, Sereceno (2004) suggested that we should pay attention to how society views children during different historical periods and also consider how issues such as race, class and culture can influence child development and portrayal in terms of social and cultural practice. Aries (1962) showed that childhood is constructed differently according to time and place. In paintings from the fifteenth and sixteenth centuries children are the same size as adults and dressed in similar clothing. Aries concluded that, in medieval society, childhood was 'not in existence'. Children were viewed as miniature versions of adults. Sereceno (2004) postulated that culture, race, social class, religion, gender, politics and education play very important roles in the way in which children experience their lives. Social discourses of childhood, whether right or wrong, tend to form the accepted view of what it is to be a child. Finally, today, isolation, abuse, exploitation, oppression and cruelty are among the factors that characterise childhood.

Chapter 3 focuses on the ways in which twins are misunderstood. Among other things, I highlight how the governmentalisation of life seemingly creates a situation whereby twins must be decontextualised in order to understand themselves and be understood by others; that is, social norms prescribe how an individual should live their life as a certain kind of person, and twins must thus deconstruct themselves as a unit in order to fit in as individuals.

3

BEING MISUNDERSTOOD

This chapter focuses on twins' first-hand accounts of being misunderstood by others, including psychologists, and of misunderstanding themselves. I argue that twins describe themselves very differently to their representations in both popular culture and the psychological literature. I further argue that the psychological ideas, social discourses and cultural representations applied to twins possibly contribute to the problem of misunderstanding oneself, which the twins discuss in their accounts.

This chapter focuses on six themes, each providing a different lens through which to analyse the concept of being misunderstood. These themes are expressions of being misunderstood; strange knowledge; marriage problems; comparison; complexity; and misunderstanding self.

Field notes and personal reflections

More than half of the twins who took part in this study describe being a twin as a complex experience that is difficult to understand. Among other things, they stated that they found it difficult to describe their feelings and experiences to me Norma, for example, stated:

> It's too complex for me to say, it's not like uhm ... this is how it really is because we know that unless you are a twin you won't really get it. There is no point in ... you know, there are many ways of knowing the truth so you leave them to it because it's easier.

Expressions of being misunderstood

Eight of the twin pairs who took part in this study expressed feelings of being misunderstood, in terms of their personal identity, close relationships; and differences and similarities. The transcripts reveal that the twins felt misunderstood as a result of how they have been treated; other people's reactions; childhood experiences; other people's beliefs about twins; how identical twins are depicted in popular culture; and the terms people use to describe them. Particular discourses, superstitions, beliefs and films are challenged, questioned and dismissed by twins in relation to the theme of being misunderstood. Three extracts focus on expressions of being misunderstood. First is Kate:

> People can argue and say I have raised two sets of twins, I have brothers or sisters who are twins, but all that means nothing when it comes to whether you understand identical twins or not. Our own parents dressed us the same, made us eat from the same plate, gave us similar names. That is enough suggestions; they think we are one person and identical in everything as in our faces, but this is not true. Our mum and dad thought they were being great parents and yes as far as they were concerned they were. But let's face it – did they give us a chance to be ourselves as two different people? They didn't. They were sincerely wrong, bless them. We were treated in a way that encouraged us to see ourselves as one person. Now we are grown up we can tell you that treatment was based on a wrong understanding.

Kate clearly believes that it is very difficult to understand twins, even for parents or siblings. She describes herself and her twin as victims, robbed of the chance to be unique individuals as a result of being misunderstood. She feels they were denied a chance to be 'themselves' as two different people and states that their parents were wrong to treat them as one entity – for example, dressing them in matching clothes and serving their meals on a shared plate – rather than individuals. Their parents failed to understand them as twins.

Next is Amanda, who stated:

> People think they know about twins but they are just far from understanding us. I think we are too complicated. You can't write books about planet Mars when you have always been on earth, can you? There is a lot being said about identical twins by ordinary

people, if you know what I mean. We told you about the twin telepathy thing and those other stupid beliefs that when she is hungry, I feel hungry too. Do you know people who write that tend to think they know twin lives and they have something to write to the world about? Yeah, it's true, they write hundreds of pages and when we as twins read, we just find out, less than a quarter of the book is true and the rest is just stories they cook up. We say okay, feel pity for the poor readers.

Amanda also feels that other people think they understand identical twins, when actually they do not, because they are 'too complicated'. Amanda believes that twins 'live in their own world', which is inexplicable to others; hence, they are misunderstood. She also identifies 'stupid beliefs', for example twin telepathy, as a source of being misunderstood. In brief, the clear message expressed by Amanda's is: identical twins are complex and difficult to understand, and those who are not twins cannot understand them.

Strange knowledge

I next focus on the theme of 'strange knowledge'. I use this term to cover the apparently odd way in which identicial twins communicate and know things about each other. Interestingly, some twins appeared to endorse and confirm the notion of twin telepathy while others dismissed it as fantasy. The extracts presented describe being misunderstood in three unique ways. First is Gloria:

> Have you ever felt … aaah, it's difficult to explain, but I think everyone has that aaah… instinct, if you like to use the word. Well, whatever they call it, I think this is the thing they mistake for twin telepathy; they give it a name when a twin feels it, but we all can know things through instinct. Do you know the song, 'I have a feeling'? That is what it's saying. Freddy Crow is the singer, but he is not a twin, yet he has it. When they talk about us, you know when people are not really talking to you and you can't even hear what they are saying but something in you feels they are talking about you and you lift your head and see someone pointing at you.

According to this extract, the notion of twin telepathy is based on a misunderstanding of twins because this 'instinct' is actually felt by all human beings.

Next is Lesley:

> If I am all right, happy, chatty, you know, playing loud music and all of that, and then suddenly something changes my mood, I become suspicious that it's a message that she is bothered. I know people around me at that time will not get that; they'll say she's moody, she changes like the weather. But guess what, I have rung her to check if she's okay when I have that feeling and found that she's not.

Lesley's extract suggests that twins are misunderstood and wrongly labelled as moody and changing like the weather when they are actually reacting to concerns about their twin's well-being. She put it in a way that indicates she has an expectation of being misunderstood as a twin.

Finally, on this same theme, Jerry states:

> People who expect us to know when one of us is unwell through some super instinct or strange methods are out of touch with the reality. It does not register to them that we are just like them; thus why we eat sandwiches and drink coke like them.

Unlike Lesley, who alludes to a strange ability to recognise if something is wrong with her twin, Jerry describes people who believe that twins have telepathic powers as 'out of touch'. In other words, they are seen as misunderstanding twins. Jerry further suggests that twins are like everyone else, which some people do not understand. He, too, feels misunderstood.

This theme has shown that the notion of twin telepathy is part of the problem associated with misunderstanding twins. Although the actual phrase 'twin telepathy' was not used to describe the strange ways in which twins claim to understand and communicate with each other, it was implied to be one way in which people misunderstand twins.

Marriage problems

Another aspect of being misunderstood as twins is reflected in the way they speak about their marriage problems. Some extracts suggest that the participant twins have experienced problems in their marriages and other romantic relationships because their partners have been unable to understand their close bond. I start with an extract from Norma:

> It's not even difficult; it's complex because he has to deal with me but at times he has to deal with the twin at the same time. Not that she is

> getting involved or anything ... he misinterprets her care and love for me. He thinks she is interfering, being nosey. I think it will take him four lives to understand that.

This extract indicates that love and care operating in twin relationships can be misconstrued as interference, which causes marital problems. The phrase 'he misinterprets' can be understood to mean 'he misunderstands'. The misunderstood twin wrongly earns the label of 'being nosey'. Above all, the extract suggests that the partner will inevitably misunderstand the twin relationship and the problem may not be resolved.

The second example on this theme is provided by Summer:

> We struggled a bit, both of us, with our partners when we started off; they could not figure out the best way to deal with us because we demanded space for each other. It gave them the impression that we were more committed to each other, we put each other first; maybe we were not interested in marriage, all that. But we are okay and happy now. There is a bit of us in both of our marriages but we can't help it, you know. At least now they know it's not what they thought in those days. [Both twins laugh]

This extract indicates that Summer and her twin sister experienced problems in the early stages of their marriages as a result of being misunderstood. The phrase 'they could not figure out the best way to deal with us' suggests an experience of being misunderstood. Also, the statement 'at least now they know it's not what they thought in those days' indicates that their partners once perceived things wrongly, which is also synonymous with being misunderstood.

Above, I have highlighted the notion that being misunderstood as a twin can cause marriage problems. I have also shown that the close relationship that exists between twins can mean one thing for the twins and another for their romantic partners. I now go on to another aspect of being misunderstood, the question of comparisons.

Comparisons

This section features identical twins being subjected to comparison by others, as a reflection of being misunderstood. It begins with an extract from Charlotte:

> You get compared loads; people want to see how similar and how different you are. I think they are trying to study something they don't understand about us.

Comparing identical twins can be understood as another way of misunderstanding them, because it is impossible to gain conclusive results from simple comparisons without taking other factors into account.

Finally, in relation to comparisons, Kate states:

> We had people compare us long before we learnt the word compare. People compared our voices, personalities, dressing, school grades – everything. We did not like it; it was frustrating. But they did not understand our position on what they were doing. We hated it, we hate it now; yet they still do it. Maybe you are the first to do formal research on us with our permission, but people started studying us long back.

This extract adopts a strong tone of displeasure in response to being mis-understood, as indicated by the phrase, 'we hated it, we hate it now'. The hatred that Kate feels in terms of these comparisons centres on feeling misunderstood.

Complexity

Being a twin is described by some of the participants as a complex experi-ence, difficult to understand, especially by those who are not twins. Amanda states:

> People think they know about twins but they are just far from understanding us. I think we are too complicated. You can't write books about planet Mars when you have always been on earth, can you?

The first part of this extract suggests that from Amanda's point of view, people misunderstand twins and are ignorant about them. The second part sheds some light on why she thinks twins are so often misunderstood: 'I think we are too complicated.'

On the issue of complexity, Norma states:

> It's too complex for me to say, it's not like uhm … this is how it really is because we know that unless you are a twin you won't really get it. There is no point in … you know, there are many ways of knowing the truth so you leave them to it because it's easier.

Norma also associates being a twin with complexity. She implies that it is not easy to understand twins, hence the strong possibility of misunderstanding them. This extract echoes Amanda's belief that, unless you have experienced life as a twin, you cannot have a comprehensive understanding of twins and will always misunderstand them.

Finally, Tony states:

> We are twins but we have a long, complicated story. We did not know each other until 13 years ago...

In this case, the complexity referred to concerns the twins' life story, which possibly affects who they are and how they do things. As a result, people might misunderstand them because they do not know this background information.

Misunderstanding the self

Besides being misunderstood by others, twins also express a failure to understand themselves. As Susan states:

> Anyway, we don't understand ourselves fully either. I think nobody understands themselves to the dot; maybe psychologists do. [Light laughter]

The phrase 'we don't understand ourselves fully' suggests that Susan and her twin misunderstand themselves to some extent. Susan does not state which aspects of themselves they struggle to understand, however. She refers to 'we', which suggests that both twins have an issue with misunderstanding themselves. At the end of the extract Susan appears to console herself by claiming that everyone struggles to understand themselves.

On the subject of misunderstanding the self, Lonnie states:

> No, we don't even understand ourselves either, so we can't expect other people to. [Both twins laugh] Sometimes we are so similar and at other times we are really different and I find that a bit difficult to understand. I can't get my head around why we can be so similar and be so different; it's the extent of difference and similarity that is a riddle for me. It's just really hard how we develop these similarities and these differences.

This extract also includes both identical twins in relation to the problem of misunderstanding self. The use of the word 'either' in the first sentence suggests that she is indirectly avoiding the possible stigma of a 'twin problem'.

In this extract, some details of why identical twins struggle to understand themselves are given; however, they are related in a way that does not include the other twin as evidenced by the use of the personal pronoun 'I'. What is clearly suggested, though, is that neither identical twin understands herself.

The last example is provided by Kasey:

> We were treated like separate extensions of one set and we believed we were for some time.

Her words show that the aspect of their lives that they do not understand is related to their identity, because there used to be a time in their lives when they thought they were extensions of one person. It is also indicated that other people's treatment of these twins contributed to their misunderstanding of themselves. The problem of misunderstanding self in twins can thus be the creation of other people around them.

In this section I have shown that twins do experience the problem of misunderstanding self. I have also highlighted that the way they speak about this issue is carefully worded to avoid the possible stigma that may result from seeing it as a 'twin problem'.

The 'wrong subjects': a discussion

Previous studies have associated the notion of being misunderstood with 'race' and ethnicity, couple relationships, religion, mental health, transgender and gay identities, and invisible disabilities (Gaillard et al., 2009). These subjects tend to be treated like the 'wrong' ethnicity in a white Western context; the 'wrong' kind of person within a relationship that is supposed to be evenly matched, even symbiotic, not broken up and fractured; the 'wrong' psyche; the 'wrong' relationship to gender and sexuality; the 'wrong' body, but in a way that people can't recognise. I argue that this wrongness is a social construction and leads to feelings of being misunderstood. The wrongness is itself the product of a prescriptive socio-cultural context that tells individuals how to 'be' in twin relationships, romantic couples and even their bodies, and how to understand the world. The twin prescription is particularly dramatic because it tells twins that they are not proper individual subjects because of their joint identity. Twins are born as a pair and often live most of their lives as a pair, with no experience of life as individuals. Identical twins who prefer to embrace their joint identity but live in Western societies that value individualism may experience feeling misunderstood because they are perceived as 'wrong individuals'. A good example of this was discussed in the section on marriage problems where, among other things, twins spoke of 'buying one and getting one for free'.

The problem of being misunderstood as addressed by identical twins in this chapter reflects and emphasises the governmentalisation of life as an individual (Rose, 1985). The themes considered in this chapter show the extent to which twins are regulated by the norms prescribing life for an individual. Thus maybe 'feeling misunderstood' is actually a kind of resistance to such norms.

The notion of an individual

The notion of individuals, dominant in Western society, creates a two-way problem that emerges across all of my analysis. It is a problem both for identical twins and others around them. The plural way in which twins speak about themselves does not fit the Western social context within which they live, which poses a problem for them and others. The problem is that being an individual seems to mean one thing for twins and another for other people. It appears that twins do think of themselves as 'individuals', albeit in a different way. A good example of departure from the hegemonic Western representation of twins and individuals is the theme of 'performance of twin identity', addressed in Chapter 2, which indicates that twins sometimes swap roles by taking advantage of their physical resemblance. However, in order to effectively swap identities and confuse people, twins need more than just their physical resemblance and often their conduct and way of doing things are uniform too. As a result, in the eyes of others, they are one and the same person. That uniformity is arguably problematic. It promotes similarity at the expense of individuality and therefore challenges the individual difference and uniqueness valued in Western culture. The very act of swapping identities suggests that twins see themselves not as unique but similar.

This is one of the areas that creates the problem of 'being misunderstood' for twins because treating them as individuals does not fit with their experiences as a couple and a pair. However, a couple, as we see in the twins' own accounts, can be used as a metaphor for understanding twins in a social context like that of Western society, where representations of individual differences are dominant and there is a strong resemblance between twins and romantic couples.

As I highlighted earlier, Western cultures emphasise individual differences and personal uniqueness; people are taught to respect individual rights and embrace individual liberty, and to reject norms and conformity. I also demonstrated that, because twins are born as a pair and live most of their life as a pair, they do not have the experience of life as individuals that is emphasised in Western culture. As a consequence, twins feel misunderstood.

Gaillard et al. (2009) explored mental health patients' experiences of being misunderstood and found that it was associated with social stigma, frustration and feeling pressured. Tomura (2009) interviewed prostitutes regarding their experiences of being misunderstood and linked it with dehumanisation and false perceptions. Appiah (2014) interviewed young black man in California and identified that being misunderstood was a complex experience, involving a sense of vulnerability and an increased chance of negative encounters with the police. The theme of complexity in this book is in line with Appiah's findings; twins describe their story as long and complicated and being a twin as a complex experience.

On the theme of comparison, the language and tone used by twins expressed their annoyance with those who compare and misunderstand them. Twins referred to the experience of being compared using words such as 'frustrating' and 'hate'. According to Condon (2008), this expression of annoyance suggests a feeling of being misunderstood. Gaillard et al. (2009) also associated frustration with being misunderstood; and Condon (2008) linked being misunderstood and misunderstanding oneself with a sense of incompleteness. Twins did state that they do not fully understand themselves. That incompleteness in understanding can imply a misunderstanding of the self when looked at in the context of Condon's work. Being taken the wrong way, which is expressed by twins when they address the issue of twin telepathy in the theme of strange knowledge, is another indication of being misunderstood when considered through the lens of Condon's work.

Appiah's (2014) report that being misunderstood for a black man in California increased chances of vulnerability, poor treatment and patronisation by the police officers implied that being misunderstood is consequential, it has implications. I suggest that being misunderstood is, for twins, a consequence of social structural arrangements in Western societies that have failed to acknowledge or appreciate the unique experiences of identical twins. Such social structures hinder attempts to accept and treat twins as individuals who are different from 'individual subjects'. If twin identity is to be understood differently, not only should researchers consider more than the biology of twins, but society as a whole must be willing to change perspective and accept education on this subject.

The way twins themselves appear to articulate the complexity of their identity from a biological perspective – as something from within. The biological perspective they seem to draw upon is evident in both popular culture and the psychological literature. Possibly twins, and wider society, gain this 'wrong' understanding of twin identity from such sources. Unfortunately, misunderstanding by others has implications for how twins are treated in their society. The theme of identity confusion highlights that: twins are treated as 'one person'. It appears that those who fail to understand and appreciate that twins are unique individuals in spite of their similar physical appearance tend to treat them the same, which in essence undermines their individuality and uniqueness. I argue that both problems – misunderstanding of twins and misunderstanding of self – are caused in part by too great an emphasis on the biological perspective in the twin studies conducted by mainstream psychologists. I further propose that the problem of misunderstanding and pathologising twins would be easily addressed if twin studies relocated their focus from the biology of twins to their social environments and relationships.

The governmentalisation of life as an individual, as highlighted by Rose (1985), fails to appreciate variation between subjects. For instance, in the case of twins, they are not recognised as both individuals and twins. It can be reasonably argued that this failure arises from misunderstanding twins. The possibility of understanding that twins are not two singletons born together but specifically 'twins' appears to be missing from the normative notion of individual subjects.

Social norms favouring the individual mean that identical twins must be removed from the context of their twinhood in order to be understood by themselves and others. This situation is a recipe for both social misunderstandings of twins by others in Western societies and misunderstanding on the part of twins themselves. Twins are born 'married'; their accounts highlight how they are an integral part of each other's lives. Their 'divorce', which is encouraged indirectly by the governmentalisation of life as individuals, can be seen as augmenting Western society's misunderstandings of twins. I argue that, if unchallenged, the governmentalisation of life as an individual causes the stigmatisation and pathologisation of twins. Other people wrongly view twins through the lens of 'fully' individual subjects and possibly see and label them as 'misfits' or, at best, as divorced individuals.

Society must appreciate that twinship is a type of exclusive partnership that. Twins themselves have to exercise patience and show empathy when communicating with people who are not twins because such people will not understand them as readily. Failure to do so on the part of twins may perpetuate the problem of being misunderstood. A twin may expect their sibling to 'just know' what they want or mean, as their accounts on the theme of strange knowledge indicate. Indeed, a twin may often understand things about their co-twin that others do not. They may even finish each other's sentences and predict each other's reactions as a result of the strength of the bond they share. To live in a broader social world, they have to be sensitive to non-twins who do not share information in the same way and ensure clear communication with them. However, their experience of twin 'understanding' may make it inevitable that 'misunderstanding' is also prominent in their experiences of that broader world.

I suggest that funding be provided to enable the findings of researchers and organisations that support and explore identical twin relationships to be applied to address the problems encountered by such twins, particularly in relation to being misunderstood and marital issues.

Chapter 4 addresses the dynamics of twin identity.

4
TWIN IDENTITY

This chapter deals with different aspects of twin identity, again by addressing various themes. I focus on this issue because twins had a great deal to say about identity. I address joint identity, twin identity as something from within, performance of twin identity, identity confusion, twin identity tied to one's name and, finally, twin identity as a social construct.

Unlike the abstract, objective ways in which traditional psychological research speaks about twin identity, in this chapter I argue that a complex web of influences, including culture and society, informs how twins construct, claim and perform their identities. I make use of my field note observations and personal reflections to clarify my argument. The first area on which I focus is my field note observations.

Being an outsider, and by that I mean a researcher, and in particular one who is not a twin and has no personal connection to twins, I think that I represented the social world to and provided an audience for the twins' performance of their identity. The performance of twin identity that I observed included: wearing the same clothes and having similar hairstyles; completing each other's sentences when giving their accounts; using 'we' and 'us' even when expressing individual opinions and describing personal feelings; and choosing similar names as pseudonyms.

Some of the twin pairs who participated in the interviews seemed to stress their similarity, not only in how they dressed but also in the way they spoke about their lives and presented themselves. I also noticed that some sets of twins sat very closely together and at times even held hands. Conversely, I observed that those twins who emphasised difference and uniqueness in their accounts dressed dissimilarly.

Another observation of these twins' behaviour concerned demonstrating how well each knew the other. When I was offered a drink, one twin would ask me if I wanted tea or coffee. That twin would then make drinks for me, herself and the other twin – without feeling the need to check what the latter wanted. That behaviour made me feel like an outsider and seemed to me a performance of similar identity, to some extent, because the way in which the drinks were offered appeared to state: 'we are twins; not only are we dressed the same but when I need a drink my twin needs one too'. I acknowledge that this may possibly happen with close friends too. However, in this context, taking into account that the twins in question had attended the interview similarly dressed, with similar hairstyles, and gave an account of their lives emphasising similarity over individuality, I categorised the incident as a performance of similarity.

Those twins who dressed differently tended to sit further apart and emphasised individuality in their accounts. They explained that they were not similar in every respect and wanted to be recognised as different and unique individuals. These were identity performances of a different kind – stressing their own personhood rather than twinship.

Joint identity

The phrase 'joint identity' is used here to refer to twin discourses emphasising similarity and shared experiences. suggesting s that twins share a joint identity. I begin with Norma's response to the interview ice-breaker question, 'What can you tell me about identical twins?' She responded:

> I am a twin … I don't know, my twin is a part of me; I can't change that and neither can she. You know what – I think she is a special part of me. We are twins; I think it's not rocket science that, since we are twins, it means we are on one page. If somebody said to me tell me about twins, this is what I would say. We are twins and we are part of each other. There are many things I can tell you depending on how you zero in on your questions. You see, when you say what can you tell me about twins you are not really specific, so I tell you what is important to me; you know, what I think answers the question. I know you're after something so feel free to ask specific questions about twins. I will do my best to give you answers.

In this extract, Norma describes herself in a way that can be understood to mean she is an extension of her twin. The language she uses indicates that she links who she is to her sister and links who her sister is to herself. Stating that she is a twin automatically identifies and connects her to another person. That to a certain degree can be understood to mean joint identity. Norma states that her twin is part of her, part of her identity.

On the theme of joint identity, Amanda stated:

> [T]o us, we are one, because we do everything together and she won't understand why one of us would say we are in trouble. Well, there are many things that people will not understand about us and this is one of them. We are one. We appreciate that you are looking at two people but the angle from which we look at ourselves is different from yours; we see ourselves through the lens of twins. We are one from that perspective. In life generally people look at things through different lenses. So what you see depends on where you are looking from. Does this drive a point? I'm only trying to explain why we think we see ourselves as one and why you probably may see us as such. Does it drive a point?

Amanda uses similar language to Norma and, again, a joint identity is claimed. Amanda's claim that she and her twin see themselves as one suggests that they do not perceive themselves as unique individuals and instead share a joint identity. Amanda mostly uses 'we' even though she is describing her own understanding of twinhood, and stresses their 'oneness' throughout. In so doing, she not only emphasises their closeness but explicitly claims that twins share a joint identity. Amanda acknowledges, however, that she does not expect everyone to see twins as one because each individual looks through a different lens.

Twin identity as something from 'within'

Here I address extracts in which twins speak in a way that suggests that their identity as twins is centred on something inside them. As Steve stated:

> I think twins are not in similar faces but in the blood. We're just connected and bonded. We are friends, very great buddies, you know; yah, its good. I personally think it's great to have a person so special to you, like your twin; you have a special relationship and they probably understand you far better than anybody else. All this

traces to what I told you before – the connection, the connection that flows in our veins makes us who we are. Other things are secondary.

Steve suggests that twin identity is predetermined by innate factors. This introduces an interesting dimension of twin identity. His statement begins by dismissing the most obvious element of identical twin identity – their similar physical appearance. Rather, he believes it is something deeper – 'in the blood'. This implies that he does not connect his identity as an identical twin to his physical appearance but instead to something inside him.
April expressed similar feelings:

> We sat next to each other and shared our food when mum had us in the womb. That tells how far, a long way, we have come together. We did not just meet; we started out together from the very beginning. All our similar experiences of life and our similar nature, if it makes sense, have shaped us to be the same. When we look in the mirror together it reminds us of our similarity. We have that in our nature; our nature is similar, we carry the same nature.

This extract shows another dimension of the claim that what makes identical twins who they are is something deeper than what people see in their physical appearance, deeper even than their experiences in life. April ascribes her similarity to her sister to what she calls 'our similar nature'. She states that it is that similar nature that makes them the same. She appreciates the influence of external forces in life but makes a stronger claim for the similarity of their nature having forged their identity. The similar nature referred to here is not something outside of them that can be seen but is something within them, having to do with being as twins.
Although no twins referred to the nature–nurture issue, they did appear to believe that their similarity was inherited and innate – inside them.

Performance of twin identity

Here, I address how twins perform their twin identity according to ime and place, through the course of their lives. First is Shalom, who stated:

> You know, me and my sister, we are typical twins … some twins are opposites. With us, my sister likes netball, she plays; I like netball, I play it. She sings, I sing; I hate football, she hates football; and we are equally

good at whatever we do, no one is better. She hates McDonald's, I hate McDonald's. I think I like the kind of guys she goes out with and she likes what I like. We basically don't go out with chubby guys, we don't hate them but we don't love them either. You can produce a list of things I like and hate by simply asking her what she likes or hates. Her list will tell you something about her, and tell you the same thing about me. That's twins for you.

Shalom begins by claiming a typical twin identity. She goes on to describe how they perform the concept of 'typical twins', stressing their similarity and sameness. It seems that Shalom and her sister perform their understanding of 'typical twins' by doing the same things and adopting similar likes and dislikes. Possibly she feels that twins who appreciate and embrace their individual differences are atypical.

Charlotte, however, provided a different view:

[We] don't force similarities on ourselves; we don't let people do it either. We just live naturally, whatever people see on us now, this is all there is. There are no artificial similarities we were raised with; we are mature now. ... At some point it was about being the same, as twins. People expected us to be the same; if you did not seem to be treading that line you were thought of as illegitimate twins. I can say we lived part of our childhood like puppets, having to reflect what people thought was right and proper for twins to do. We don't now; we don't force any similarities on us and no one can do that anymore. We are now mature and what you see is what you get. We live our lives naturally; no added flavours.

This extract indicates that Charlotte and her twin refuse to perform an artificial similarity to reflect the stereotypical twin identity, which seems to be what other people expect from them. Further reading shows that, at some point in their lives, Charlotte and her twin performed an imposed similarity because of the way they had been reared as children. The word 'artificial' suggests that the similarities were not natural to them but cultivated. However, as mature twins this performance of identity changed, from artificial and imposed to natural, suggesting that twins can alter how they perform at different stages of their development. It also indicates that changes in the home and social environment may alter what it is to be a twin – and how twins perform being twins can also change as a result.

Identity confusion

Here, I focus on identity confusion in two ways. First, I address the suggestion (made by a number of the twins) that other people confuse their identity and, second, I consider twins' feelings about their confused identity.
On the issue of identity confusion, Lesley stated:

> We share our identity. We get our names swapped around, and it's not nice sometimes. When people get mixed up about who is who between us they impose confusion on us. I don't like that a bit. I appreciate it's not easy to tell us apart, so I put up with it. So, yah, we share who we are, we share our names, we share our identity This has been going on since we were toddlers; people would not make an effort to tell us apart, they would just call out one of our names. Some would just say 'twins' to conceal that they could not tell who is who. All this was not too bad but what was disgusting was being blamed for another's wrongs. Kids who had hitches with her at school would pick a fight with me later thinking it was me. The other side of the coin was the nicer one, though it rarely came about; I would get compliments for the good she did. I liked that part. [All laugh]

This extract suggests that theidentity confusion experienced by identical twins is generated by other people's failure to tell them apart. The swapping of their names by others also creates a degree of identity confusion. Lesley does, however, state that she and her twin share their identity, which may be another source of the confusion they experience. Overall, the tone of her narrative indicates Lesley's displeasure at the identity confusion resulting from swapping of the twins' names.
Addressing the same issue, Shalom stated:

> I think people think we are the same person and that gives me a head-ache because we are not. You might easily, very easily, fall into the trap of thinking common sense exists in every head but it doesn't. Unfortunately, it doesn't. I personally think it's common sense that each person is different but amazingly that is not how some people think, especially if you are a twin. Some people think she is me and I am her. Whatever way they take it, it is so mixed up. Their take is that twins means you are one person, you are the same; there is no uniqueness in you because your faces, body structure and all looks

are identical. I put up with people mixing up our names but when it comes to whether we are one person or not, that confusion gives me a terrible headache.

Here, identity confusion is not related to the swapping of names but is centred instead on what others think about twins – that they are 'the same person'. Obviously, twins are not one person; they are two unique individuals. Like Lesley's, the tone of this extract indicates displeasure. Shalom's belief that people treat twins as one person may be understood as a metaphor for failure to respect twins' individual differences and uniqueness and treating them as the same.

The flipside of this aspect of identity confusion is also linked with the fact of twins themselves being confused about their own identity. For example, Amanda stated:

[T]o us, we are one, because we do everything together and she won't understand why one of us would say we are in trouble. Well there are many things that people will not understand about us and this is one of them. We are one. We appreciate that you are looking at two people but the angle from which we look at ourselves is different from yours, we see ourselves through the lens of twins. We are one from that perspective. In life, generally people look at things through different lens. So, what you see depends on where you are looking from. Does this drive a point? Am only trying to explain why we think we see ourselves as one and why you probably may see us as such. Does it drive a point?

Amanda and her twin are possibly confused about their own identity as twins, and indeed speak of themselves as one. Describing themselves as being in trouble when incident affects only one of them may be seen as identity confusion but can also be understood as an expression of closeness and loyalty to one another.

Lonnie described her own experience of identity confusion thus:

We were treated like separate extensions of one set and we believed we were for some time. You know when everyone just calls you twins, it's like you don't have names; if you do, they are not as important – what matters is twins. Everything was about twins in our world, never two similar looking but different sisters; it was about how similar we are, same this and same that, same dresses, same plates, sometimes not even same but one big plate. This was the treatment we received, and thus how we viewed things. We indeed at some point thought, we are somehow in some way extensions of one person, something like that. We were confused by our upbringing.

This extract clearly indicates twins' confusion concerning their own identity. The similar treatment that Lonnie and her twin sister received affected their perception of who they really were. For a while they actually believed that they were not individuals but extensions of each other, which created problems in terms of their individual identities.

Twin identity tied to one's name

Here, I consider extracts in which twins speak of themselves in a way that puts their name at the centre of their identity. Amanda, for example, stated:

> Obviously, I will start with my name, clarify that I am a twin. I always mention that you buy one and get one for free. This is to make sure that when you want to cause drama you are not dealing with one person; my twin is my partner in crime as well. We come as a pair; we come as a team; there is nothing about me without her and nothing about her without me. [Laughs] So yes, you buy yourself one; the other one will be given for free. If you don't like the other, leave both. [Laughs] This is the life we live; we do everything together. Nature paired us; you need to obey Mother Nature. If you were born paired, work well as a pair together and be naughty together. There was a time when we were very naughty; people got double trouble if they crossed our paths.

Responding to the question of how she would describe herself to someone who has never met her before, Amanda said she would obviously start with her name. Her use of the word 'obviously' at the start of the sentence indicates that Amanda takes it for granted that one's name is central to personal identity. She implies that one's name serves as the foundation upon which everything else about personal identity is built.

Steve's response to the same question is as follows:

> My name is Steve King, I have a twin brother, I live in York, I love Yorkshire pudding, I like being around my brother, I am an easygoing person – yeah, all that. [Yawns] I love people, I'm a sociable guy. I go for drinks where people are just to meet and talk. People always get our names the other way around. Many lads who drink

with us cross wires when it comes to who I am. They call my brother Steve and me him. He does not need to be out with me to get called by my name.

Here, again, the importance of one's name is stressed. Although other important details are mentioned in the extract, Steve is very careful to start with his full name. Steve clearly connects his identity with his name.

Amy provided another example on this theme:

We share our identity, we get our names swapped around, and it's not nice sometimes. All the twins I know get that; one of the things you will have to accept is being called by a wrong name. People struggle to identify us. People who we have been around for years still make mistakes. We got that at school and we're still getting it at uni.

Amy puts the concepts of identity and name side by side. To her, they are equally important. Amy sees the swapping of names as synonymous with the swapping of one's personal identity.

Twin identity as a social construct

Here, twins speak about their identity as a product of their social context. On this theme, Lesley stated:

We see ourselves as two different people who look identical but are under pressure to act similar. People would not walk up to you and say why are you trying to be different. But that treatment spoke volumes. It's difficult to break this down but we were put under pressure by the way things were at that time around us; the way our community, peers, teachers, everybody, including our parents, understood twins.

In this extract, the twins are pressured to act in a similar manner, but that pressure does not come from within. External forces, relating to the social context, are actively involved in shaping the twins' identity in a particular way. In this example, the similarity stereotype is imposed on them. Kate added:

In this country, identical twins are brainwashed; everyone makes them believe that they have to be the same in everything else like in their faces.

[Both laugh] I personally believe that most identical twins are no more similar naturally than they were made or trained to be. I rest my case.

According to this extract, 'everyone' is collectively involved in shaping twins' identity – 'brainwashing' them, as Kate sees it. Social structures and cultural norms can thus be seen as informing twin identity; people see them in a certain way and want them to behave accordingly.

Kate went on to say:

People expect us to be the same, eat the same dishes, same amount, go everywhere together. That will not be expected from people you consider normal. I very much doubt it! I wish people around here would give us a break, let us be who we are. People have their values and culture and we have our own values and they don't include being the same. I think if you are born somewhere like here, where they think twins should be the same, they don't expect you to go any other way but theirs. You are expected to follow suit. I think I am different to my sister. Some twins are way too old-fashioned. They can't get it from us. No chance, we are similar and different that's all.

This extract suggests that twin identity is performed within the context and confines of particular social expectations, which relate to all aspects of their lives.

Notions of both couples and individuals are clearly articulated throughout this chapter. Notably, on the theme of joint identity twins spoke about being a special part of each other, linking who they are to another person, being one and doing everything together. In Chapter 3 I covered how describing themselves in that way can cause identical twins to be misunderstood in Western cultures that promote individualism. Elements of this kind of talking, which connects one twin's identity to that of the other twin and thus portrays them as a single unit, emerged for the first time in Chapter 3 across all the themes addressed. Performance is another factor that carries over from that chapter. Interviewees described how they performed as 'typical twins' – by sharing common interests, for example, something which is also part of the popular representation of couples. Indeed, Seymour-Smith and Wetherell (2006) described how heterosexual couples perform and manage their 'coupleness' in similar ways to identical twins.

Goffman (1959) argued that people perform their identities in a theatrical and dramatic manner. He further suggested that people are like actors on a stage; their actions are not necessarily expressive of their unique personalities but, rather, expressions of their social roles. The performance of twin identity can be seen from the perspective of Goffman; the interviewees describing wearing the same clothes to both emphasise their twinhood and conform to social expectations of them, and talked of 'impersonating' each other.

On a different note, Butler (1997) argued that identity is a product of social construction. One identical twin in my study described feeling brainwashed as a result of being made to believe that she and her twin must be the same in every respect. She applies social constructionist theory to her own experience and clearly feels that twins are no more similar naturally than non-twins and have been made or trained to be so by those around them. Socialisation is thus seen as a tool to promote and enforce the performance of similarity in twin identity.

The theme of twin identity as something from within is in harmony with the views of Cattell (1966), who argued that identity can also be a product of child-rearing. His assumption is that people do not act out or manage the impression they give to others; they have only one true identity. That identity is synonymous with their disposition and they identify completely with it. In the extracts in this chapter the interviewees repeatedly described twinship as being 'in the blood' and stressed their similar 'natures'.

Conclusion

This chapter has shown that, contrary to the abstract, ostensibly objective ways in which psychological research speaks about twin identity, a complex web of influences, including cultural and societal factors, informs how twins construct and claim their identities. Furthermore, I have shown that there is a contradiction in the ways in which twins perceive themselves and speak about their identity. I have offered examples where some say they were special and unique while others say they are ordinary, like everyone else.

I have also shown that there are different aspects of twin identity that show how twins claim and perform their identity. Above all, I have highlighted the interesting contradictions inherent in the way twins speak of themselves and claim their identities. Chapter 5 looks at twins from the perspective of couples.

5
COUPLES

This chapter organises the material around the themes that emerged in my review of the academic literature and popular culture. One of the aims of this chapter is to highlight the way in which twins seem to account for their twinship using the representational frame of couples. Crucially, this chapter also draws attention to aspects of the research material that have enabled me to make the link between what twins say and their cultural context. I argue that twins possibly draw from couple discourses in the way that they talk about themselves. I further argue that the notion of a couple as a metaphor can be used to solve the problems of misunderstanding twins on the part of others and twins struggling to understand themselves. However, it needs to be noted that drawing on the notion of couples creates other problems because twins are, of course, not exactly like couples.

This chapter addresses a gap in the research on identical twins by looking at how they make use of couple discourses. There seems to be a strong tendency, not noted before, for twins to describe their relationship in terms resembling discourses about couples.

I will present some extracts from the twins' interviews, in order to demonstrate the ways in which they describe themselves in a way that draws on couple discourses. I will also reflect on the way I conducted the interviews, showing how that could have affected how the twins spoke of themselves as couples.

I am aware that aspects of this chapter – and some themes in particular – do not exclusively identify with romantic couples only; however, I have opted to use romantic couples as a framework because, as Kitzinger (2008) argued, romantic couples appear to be the norm from which other couples are understood. On the same note, Roseneil (2006) suggested that with the rise of heterosexual cohabitation, other relationships have generally also been depicted in terms that follow the framework of heterosexual cohabiting and married couples.

Notably, I am not treating each theme as a self-sufficient element; what is important is how all these themes link together and produce one image that resembles a romantic couple. If these themes were considered separately, as different elements, one would miss the way in which twins operate to construct the metaphor of a romantic couple. I further acknowledge that some of the elements can be described and linked together in ways other than those I describe here and in relation to other types of couple. I have chosen to link them to a romantic couple, however, because, although some of these themes can be found in other types of couple, all of them can more often be found in romantic couples; indeed, while all of them, as a set, do not describe any other kind of couple in the same way.

In this chapter I will briefly outline some aspects of my field notes as a starting point because they show how couple discourses operate in the context of twin relationships. The phrase 'couple themes' has been adopted in this chapter to refer to all aspects of identical twins' talk about their lives that reflects the influence of romantic couple discourses. This chapter features many themes that reflect a possible influence of couple discourses on twins, from various perspectives. One of the dominant ways in which people talk about relationships in Western culture concerns the connection between one person and another. Both twin and couple relationships are enacted through the flow of social and cultural discourses; I will draw on these to show some of the similarities between the ways in which twins and couples operate.

The themes that emerged from my analysis are: bonds, teaming-up, joint ownership, power relations, similarity, companionship, interdependence and, finally, jealousy. I will explain what I mean by each theme as I introduce it. From a set of occurrences from each theme in the interviews, I have selected a few, using them as examples for my analysis. The selection of extracts I use here was based on the level of expressiveness, prominence and clarity.

I had noticed a performance of 'coupleness' in twins from the time of recruitment for this study, through the course of the interviews and after the interviews, in varying ways. I will show how this performance happened in three stages, starting with the recruitment period, moving on to the course of the interviews, and concluding after the interviews. It is important to note that I reinforced the performance of coupleness in twins, as my advertisement for the study used the term 'looking for sets of twins'; that is, I had asked to see them as couples and I had interviewed them in one place, at the same time, again like a couple.

Identical twins responded to my advertisement as couples. Of the 14 twin pairs who took part in this study, I communicated with 11 on the phone, 2 via email and 1 face to face in order to confirm their participation, provide details on the venue and address any questions related to the information sheet they had already received.

I spoke to some of the twins on the phone and, in each conversation, one twin played the role of the main speaker and represented the other. For example, whenever the phone was on the loud speaker, one twin would speak to me, ask questions and discuss possible interview dates, while the other listened somewhat passively, making only short remarks and seemingly agreeing with what the other twin said. Even in those cases where both twins were actively involved in the conversation, I noticed that one twin always played the leading role in the conversation and made the key decisions. This pattern was evident in all of the conversations, to varying degrees. I have come to see this dynamic as an example of the existence of power relations within twinships, similar to those evident in couples.

Despite these observations about power relations, which appeared to suggest that one twin tends to have more power than the other, I bore in mind that this dynamic may change according to context. Maybe the twins swap roles in different conversations.

My email exchanges followed a similar pattern. Though I would write one email to each twin and send them separately, they always responded jointly, in one email, and used 'we' and 'us' throughout. Whoever wrote, wrote on behalf of both siblings. This way of representing each other also operates in couple relationships.

In one case, I actually encountered one of my subjects in a lift; he was holding a book entitled *The Story of Twin Siblings*. I started a conversation with him based on that book and later established that he was an identical twin. After talking some more, he told me that he and his brother would be interested in participating in my study, without having spoken to his brother about this yet. Later that day, he sent an email confirming that both twins would be happy to take part in my study. To me, this was another manifestation of the possible influence of couple discourses on twins and of the issue of power relations between them; one twin played the role of the main speaker and made decisions on behalf of both of them and the other seemed to just agree. I am aware that a discussion may have taken place regarding the decision to participate, that I was not privy to. However, based on what I observed, this appeared to be a power relations issue.

Some of the themes that I discuss in this chapter, for example the bond between identical twins, were evident throughout the course of the interviews and clearly reflected the influence of couple discourses. This influence on twins manifested itself in various ways, including: sitting very close to each other, their bodies touching; holding hands while sitting and talking to me; putting an arm over each other's shoulders; using 'we' and 'us' in their accounts; and using body language and other gestures, including facial expressions, in ways that made sense to them, as a couple, but were meaningless to me, as an outsider. Sometimes twins would even complete each other's sentences. All these elements bring to mind a couple, because couple relationships also feature similar bonds and expressions of closeness.

It is important to note that, while I respected the autonomy of each twin as an individual, I was more interested in their experiences and the way they accounted for themselves as twins; hence my decision to conduct joint interviews. Besides, because the interviews were conducted in their homes and I was a complete stranger, I thought that the interview environment would be more relaxed and comfortable if both twins were present. I also wanted to address the issue of power imbalance and to observe the dynamics between them. Above all, I assumed that it would be difficult for twins not to think of each other when answering my questions, and separating them could thus have a negative effect on the quality of the interviews.

The bond between twins

Thirteen of the twenty-eight identical twins interviewed in this study spoke about the bond that existed between them. Interesting statements and words are adopted by identical twins to express their bond and attachment to each other. I cite some such below.

First is Steve:

> We talk a lot, spend time together; our bond has been growing at a shocking rate. We are so much into each other, probably like all proper twins. ... [Y]ou have a special relationship and they probably understand you far better than anybody else ... the connection that flow in our dveins makes us who we are.

Steve's observation that his bond with his twin is growing seems to imply that different levels of bond operate in twin relationships. Maybe bonds can change over time. He identifies the key contributors to that bond as spending time together and talking. He also suggests that something in their blood plays a role in their bond. Steve places a strong emphasis on that bond and refers to both his twin and their relationship as 'special'. The final part of the statement can be understood as attributing the special relationship to bonding because Steve says it derives from the inborn connections that are in their blood.

Steve talks about himself and his twin in a way that suggests a possible influence of couple discourses; for example, he describes being so much into each other, spending time together and being connected; repeatedly uses 'we', 'our' and 'us'; and mentions their deep and continuous communication – 'we talk a lot'.

On the theme of the bond shared by twins, Tom stated:

> We feel attached and connected; this is how it has always been. We have never appreciated people who come between us. I would put it this way – we feel connected. I have said that I think there is something about twins that kind of links, webs you together emotionally, mentally, physically. It's one of those things you can't so easily tell another person; you need to be in it to know it. I talk to people, you know people ask questions about twins, and the answer I have given to most of them is one I am about to give you. You ready for it? [Laughs] Okay, this is the answer: if you're not a twin, you just won't get it!

The possible impact of couple discourses can be seen here too. Tom suggests that the bond between himself and his twin is characterised by mutuality, connection, attachment and jealousy – all of which may be equally applied to a romantic couple relationship.

Expressing similar views about this bond, Kate stated:

> We grew up very close, we shared, we did all things together and we were encouraged to do so both at home and outside, directly and indirectly.

Kate, too, uses phrases that suggest that identical twins draw on romantic couple discourses to understand and speak of their bond and closeness.

Kate also appears to identify a developmental aspect of bond; that they result from sharing and doing things together. The influence of couple discourses began, she feels, when they were growing up and were cultivated and promoted in their social context. This extract sheds some light on what could be the basis of twin bonds. Unlike Steve, who attributed the bonds to something in their blood, Kate feels that social factors play a key role. She also mentioned sharing, which, although she did not say it, might include sharing the prenatal environment.

To explain her views on the bond she shares with her twin, April explained:

> We sat next to each other and shared our food when mum had us in the womb. That tells how far we have come together. We did not just meet; we started out together from the very beginning…our similar nature, if it makes sense, has shaped us to be the same.

April does not use the word 'bond' but nevertherless implies it. She mentions companionship in the womb but goes on to suggests that their similar nature is what connects them rather than 'their blood', as Steve initimated. The outstanding thing about April's extract is that she is the only interviewee to suggest that 'something in twins' predetermines what they become – their similar nature is what 'shaped them'. The statement appears to disregard the role of social factors in the 'shaping' of twins.

Teaming up

Here, I address aspects of the interviews in which twins speak about themselves as functioning as a team. Of the 28 identical twins, 7, all female, said they adopt a team approach with their twin in dealing with different issues of everyday life.

The influence of romantic couple discourses is again evident in the twins' descriptions of their team approach to life.

First is Amanda:

> Obviously, I will start with my name, clarify that I am a twin, I always mention that you buy one and get one for free. This is to make sure that when you want to cause drama you are not dealing with one person; my twin is my partner in crime as well. If you don't like the other, leave both. There was a time when we were very naughty; people got double trouble if they crossed our path.

Although this extract begins with Amanda talking about who she is, she also provides some rich material on the theme of teaming up. Her statement, 'you buy one and get one for free', in this context can be understood to imply partnering, friendship and companionship. It also suggests that directly dealing with one twin means also dealing indirectly with the other – they cause drama together. In terms of functioning in daily life, Amanda refers to her twin as her partner. Her use of that word, which paints a picture of a couple gives further grounds to suggest that twins draw from couple discourses in the way they talk about their lives.

Jackie has this to say about teaming up:

> [A]s identical twins we tend to love being around each other and doing things together. When we were kids, we did not have the word 'mine' in our usage. Our chest of drawers, whatever was there, when I say that I mean from them bloody knickers under our skirts to the hats on top of our heads, was just for the twins. I had nothing; she had nothing. Stuff belonged to us. Anyone could pick anything. We lived like that most of our childhood.

This extract is interestingly embedded with phrases that imply teaming up in different ways in the lives of twins. For example, Jackie's observation that she and her twin 'love being around each other and doing things together' can be seen as implying the coupling, partnering and joining together of individuals who then become a unit – which is teaming up. Her repeated use of the words 'we', 'our' and 'us' also suggests that they work together as a team or unit.

Claire provided a different perspective on the teaming up of identical twins:

> It's like if one of us is in trouble, we gang up to defend each other, even if we are in the wrong. We always stand by each other and people tend to think we are a bunch stuck together because of that. I think we are a winning team. [Laughs] We don't lose arguments; we can talk for England. We talk until the next person shuts their ugly mouth up. I know other twins who do that. I have seen lots and lots on movies, twins gang up. They fight each other's wars. From experience, I think it makes life easier. I'm glad I'm a twin. It's super. It's a great deal.

Claire emphasised the loyalty that may exist in a twin team. She describes their 'winning team' in almost military terms – as a *unit* that *gangs up* and *fights wars*. She views teaming up as standing by each other, in all circumstances – as do many, if not all, romantic couples.

Joint ownership

Joint ownership was clearly an issue for the identical twins I interviewed. They mentioned shared toys and clothes, and joint identity, including being collectively called 'the twins', 'the boys' or 'the girls' and not by their own names. Below, I cite some examples of joint ownership.

I start with an extract from Jackie:

> Everything was bought in pairs, at the same time and mostly same colours and makes. You might think we had issues trying to tell stuff apart but we never tried to. We called stuff ours. All we needed was two pairs of stuff, it did not matter what belonged to whom. Stuff belonged to us; we were happy to share. [Laughs]

The extract explicitly states that everything belonged to both twins, which implies joint ownership. The statement indicates that Jackie's parents had a role in this joint ownership; indeed, they may have cultivated through buying clothing that was difficult to identify as belonging to one or other twin. Joint ownership was a form of socialisation imposed on these twins when they were very young; they simply accepted it as the norm.

Kate, too, described joint ownership in positive terms:

> No one owned anything; everything between us was ours. We gladly shared everything, including underpants. [Both laugh] Twins share; we share who we are. Our life has been about us; never me, never her. All she ever had I could call mine and freely use for myself; all I ever had you know she could call hers and use as she pleased. Things have always been that way. I am not a twin without her; we owe who we are to each other.

Joint ownership is referred to here both explicitly and implicitly, and includes not only possessions but also identity. Kate states that she is not a twin without her sister, which can be interpreted as meaning that a twin identity is not possible unless shared jointly with another person. Kate echoes the previous extracts but uses stronger language: 'No one owned anything.' Interestingly, however, she refers to joint ownership in the past tense, inferring that this is no longer the case in their adult lives.

My last example under this theme is provided by Charlotte:

> Your clothes are not just yours alone; they are for us. We share our identity. We get our names swapped around, and it's not nice sometimes.

Charlotte, too, infers that joint ownership of possessions equates to a shared identity. She also mentions speaks of her relationship with her twin sister in a way that shows not only their close relationship but also an element of identity confusion resulting from their similar physical appearance and the swapping of their names by others. Charlotte appears to understand identity as centred on one's name. To continue the couple metaphor, married couples generally share a surname as a symbol of their new joint identity; maybe because it is their own choice, rather than imposed on them, it is something to be celebrated rather than railed against.

Power relations

Of the 28 identical twins who took part in this study, 6 raised power relations issues. Five used words and phrases indicating that they occupied the less powerful position in their twinship, including 'dominated', 'having to follow suit', 'having to obey' and 'feeling like the other twin was the ring-leader'. Only one twin suggested they were the 'main player'.

The phrase 'power relations' is applied here to the themes of 'dominance and being dominated', issues that feature in identical twins' observations about their relationships. Power relations have been described in the literature pertaining to romantic couples and may thus inform identical twins view of their own relationship.

Amy provides the first example:

> More than half the time, she would give me those toys she was not interested in playing with and I would take them. So, I think she dominated me. Mum has told us I was always an underdog. Well, she still does in clever ways now. Well, this is how life goes anyway; if you put people together, somebody's ideas will be influential and will come top – they will dominate the group. Animals in the jungle have some bits of that too for order. I think I was smart enough not to pick a fight over a toy. [All laugh] I think she wanted to dominate and I wanted peace, so I let her. [Laughs]

Amy describes her position in the twin relationship in unequivocal terms: 'dominated' and 'underdog'. It is striking that Amy, a mature woman, still feels that her twin occupies a dominant position, suggesting that power remains an issue into adulthood. How that dominance is played out may change – more subtly, in 'clever ways' – but it is still a feature of the relationship.

My second example is provided by Lonnie:

> We fight over opinions and plans now and then. I used to follow whatever she wanted us to do but I don't now. You know when you feel like she is

> telling you where we are going on Friday night, what are we watching on tele, what we are wearing if we are going out – you feel like she is controlling you. [Laughs] One day, she made plans. We were supposed to go to Newport and she finalised everything – it was a twenty-first. When she mentioned it, she expected me to follow suit but I said, wait a minute. We clashed. I was reluctant to go but she was determined to take me along. Eventually she went on her own, which was very unusual. [Both laugh loudly] The point is, we clash over opinions and plans because she tries to dominate me. She expects me to follow suit but I don't. She thinks I'm silly but I think she's sillier. [All laugh]

Unlike in Amy's account, where a power imbalance continues into adulthood, here change has occurred post-childhood. It would have been very interesting to discover at what stage of their lives Lonnie began to resist being dominated, despite the conflict doing so created, and what factors triggered that change in behaviour.

Mary provided the final example on this theme:

> [S]he says I am a control freak. Yeah, she always says that when I want us to do things. You know what I call her? [Both laugh] Eeeh, is it okay to say it? Alright, I will say it. [Giggles] Eeeh, not in a bad way though, get my point right there, but I think she is a humble junk. [All laugh]

This extract is unique in that power issues are made clear through labelling. One twin is positioned in the relationship as a *control freak* and the other as a *humble junk*. It also highlights that if one twin assumes the role of leader the other is forced into the role of follower.

Positioning twins as opposites, controller and controlled, relates to a romantic heterosexual couple in a way because they too are opposites – male and female. Twins talking about their lives in this way, particularly the element of opposites, can be understood as drawing from heterosexual couples.

Similarity

Of the 28 participant twins, 6 female and 2 male twins expressed their views and feelings regarding their similarity to their twin. The similarities referred to range from physical appearance to hobbies, dress code, general attitude and approach to life.

First is Amina:

> We are not different that's for sure, not even one bit. We are the same, we are not different, we listen to the same music, associate with the same friends, we have the same taste for everything, if you know what I mean. We are the same in everything, everything … we both enjoy dancing and singing. It's very easy for us to tell you how similar we are than to tell you how different we are. It's very easy for a stranger to look at us and tell how similar we are than for a person who knows us to tell how different we are.

Amina's extract is interesting because she opens with a disclaimer against difference and personal uniqueness, seemingly to indirectly emphasise similarity. Her claim that nothing about them is differentmay appear exaggerated but can also be understood as implying an even higher degree of similarity between them than is possibly the case.

Amanda also stressed the strength of twin similarity:

> We are just the same. We are individuals, in that she can sit there and me here, but practically we are one. Identical twins means identical twins. It's people who share the same blood information, DNA, do you understand. It's people who came from one seed. It's people who look the same. If we want to be real, really real, me and my sister are just the same.

Amanda sees the identity of identical twins as being almost one person; she does not mention her individual identity. Overall, the language Amanda uses to describe similarity paints a picture of individuals who share almost everything in common.

The second example is from April, who says:

> All our similar experiences of life and our similar nature, if it makes sense, have shaped us to be the same. … We have that in our nature; our nature is similar, we carry the same nature.

April highlights similar experiences of life and their 'nature' as key to the similarity in twins. Nature in this context can be understood as referring to innate biological factors. It suggests that April is drawing, consciously or unconsciously, from the nature–nurture debate in order to understand her similarity to her sister. She appears to attribute similarity to their shared environment in the womb and their genes.

Companionship

Of the 28 identical twins who participated in this study, one man and six women described the experience of twinship as never being alone. That is what companionship refers to.

Charlotte provided my first example on this theme:

> The great thing is that someone is always there; you never walk alone. You have a great friend you can count on. We like our bond. I think somehow, somewhere we were wired with the same wires and that connects us; that makes us great friends, great companions. My best friend is always here. A long way back before I knew about friends, she sat right there next to me in mummy's tummy giving me hugs. [All laugh] Yes, she has been there for me. She is still here and I make sure I am always there for here.

Charlotte uses phrases that imply the existence of companionship in different ways and to different degrees. The statement 'you never walk alone' implies a relationship that features not only companionship but also loyalty and friendship. Charlotte values very highly the companionship in her twin relationship, describing it as a 'great thing' and her twin as a 'great friend'. She also intimates that, with a twin, you always have a helper, someone who is readily available to 'walk' with you through the journey of life. In addition, the extract shows that their companionship is unique because it began in the womb and has continued thereafter.

On the theme of companionship, Kasey stated:

> We are so close and we are not closer to any other person as we are close to each other. We are best friends to ourselves; we are not as close to our dad, brother, mum and our other two sisters. I think it's because we have best friends in each other. This is one of the so many very good things about being a twin – you don't meet your best friend at school; you meet your best friend in the womb. I think that's awesome; she is an awesome sister and an awesome friend. I was never lonely from the womb. [Both laugh] She was there, and mum too of course was there, but she gave me hugs and kisses before mum did. If I could choose, I would choose to be a twin again. [Laughs]

In this extract, the companionship appears to be based upon the special friendship and closeness that exists in the relationship of twins. However, there is a possibility that companionship might be the foundation from which friendship and closeness developed. There appears to be something special about the companionship of twins in that it involves a relationship that seems to be mutually satisfying and intimate.

My final example is provided by Jackie:

> We followed each other wherever and whenever. We were like shadows of each other. A shadow never leaves you; it's just there whenever and wherever. We lived that life where if you saw one of us you knew the other will just appear [Both laugh] It was great. I'm reminded of the novel about the faithful shadow; I read it years ago. The book was about a man who had a dog, and the dog was always with him and he talked of him as his shadow because it was always there. I think she has been like my dog. [All laugh]

The relationship described by Jackie indicates companionship based on mutuality, flexibility and consistency. Jackie talks only in the past tense, which suggests that their companionship changed as they grew up. Jackie's comparison of her sister to a faithful dog in a novel demonstrates that she valued that element of their relationship.

Interdependence

Six of the 28 identical twin participants, all female, said that they live and function interdependently. They suggested that they each have strengths and weakness that complement those of the other twin. The combination of the pair's parallel abilities benefitted both twins.

I cite and analyse some extracts below, in which identical twins speak about their lives as interdependent.

On this theme, Kate stated:

> [S] is North Pole, I am South Pole. We are different but we make our world spin together. We are specialist in our own areas; she drives some ends and I drive some. We are both not experts in everything but we are smart; I think we are smart because we can work as a little team and achieve great things. We need each other, we utilise each other to the max and we get things. I know where she shines and she knows me. We are pretty much different and we know how to use that to our best advantage. I think we are smart. [All laugh]

How this extract is constructed suggests that Kate seems to credit these twins' ability to function interdependently to their differences. Kate began by comparing their differences to the two poles before asserting 'we make our world spin together'. She appears to be suggesting that identical twins can be totally different but that difference does not affect their relationship negatively; instead, this difference works to the advantage of both twins and plays a key role in their interdependence; it helps them to complement each other in the way they function. Above all, Kate appears to think that it is a wise thing for them to function by having each twin focusing on what they are good at because it makes their dependence on each other effective.

On the theme of interdependence, Amy commented:

> She has that side which I don't have, and I have this side which she doesn't, but we combine that to make things happen. So, this is what I mean, how does one understand why it will take a combination of two people to make a perfect whole? It's like where I get stuck she takes over and where she gets stuck I take over. Farfetched as it sounds, it's true. That's the reason I am saying people will not understand twins. I don't even understand why I am the laid back one either. Most of the time, if we have to speak she does the talking.

Amy uses many words to articulate what Kate expressed in one sentence. This extract still centres, however, on the way in which identical twins can take advantage of their differences in order to function interdependently, each focusing on what they are good at. Amy seems to suggest that interdependence relies on their ability to recognise and appreciate what each is good at or struggles with. Amy also suggests that people will not understand this aspect of twins lives; in relation to the Western ideal of individualism, twin behaviour goes against the norm.

My last example is provided by Amanda:

> But to us, we are one, because we do everything together and she won't understand why one of us would say we are in trouble ... I will tell you why; we help each other. Like everyone, when you get into trouble you need people to help you; we have each other. We depend on each other for so many things; the correct way actually is to say we depend on each other for everything. Because of that, when one of us is in trouble, we are in trouble because we solve it together.

Amanda describes herself and her sister as being 'one'. This word ties them together as a unit and can be understood as suggesting interdependence in their functioning. Other words and phrases she uses to refer to doing things together also imply interdependence to some degree. Like Amy, Amanda also mentions the possibility of not being understood and she connects it directly to their interdependence. The last part of the extract makes it very clear that these twins depend on each other for everything. Amanda's observation that they help each other when they are in trouble implies loyalty, love and faithfulness.

In this section I have shown how the notion of interdependence between identical twin can be likened to that between romantic couples. Indeed, these twins, and other people, may use the romantic couple discourse to frame and explain the interdependent aspect of their relationship.

Jealousy

Three female participants spoke about jealousy as an aspect of their relationship. Here, this word refers to identical twins feeling offended and envious when one of them enters into a romantic relationship; it also describes the feelings of non-twins who feel excluded by the close relationship between their identical twin siblings.

I start with an extract from Jackie:

> I am still not sure whether I was jealous or I was fighting loneliness, but I hated the whole thing. I felt like, this bastard, where on earth did he come from? I made sure Sue knew how I felt because we had no secrets. She continued [with the relationship] but eventually backed out because I was not happy. I just had a bad feeling about it. Have you ever had a bad feeling about something? You know, I just had a bad feeling. I did not like it and I made it clear to her ... she knew I was not impressed. As I said, it's not easy to say why but I think I was a bit jealous; probably I was. Jealousy is a bad feeling also but there are many things that start with a bad feeling so you can't be sure; you can't be sure.

Though Jackie does not explicitly admit that she was jealous of her twin's romantic relationship, there are clear indications that she was. For example, she refers to her twin's relationship as a 'thing', calls the boyfriend a 'bastard' and describes her own sense of unhappiness. This may be understood as an indication that the relationship between some identical twins is so special and interdependent that they are terrified of losing it.

On this theme, Norma stated:

> She asks why we [twins] are closer to each other than to her and I think she doesn't accept that this is how it is. Sometimes when people

speak the tone tells you; when she asks the tone tells she is jealous. She wishes she was so close to us as we are to each other or she feels it's unfair. And everybody knows life has never been fair. Bless her, she has not lived long enough to see it but life is never fair.

Here, the non-twin sibling is described as feeling jealous of the twins' closeness and possibly excluded. Interestingly, Norma interprets more than her sister's words and also describes her 'narrative tone' as revealing her jealousy. The younger sister's jealousy seems to be motivated by the desire to be close to her twin sisters.

April provided the final example on this theme:

We had this and that to sort out at first when we met our partners because they always felt they come second but they have come to accept that they are not ordinary seconds but they are second best. We are the first ladies. [All laugh] All it is, yah, all it is; that was jealousy. [All laugh again] That's exactly what it was. Poor lads felt we give each other priority not them and their hearts were going raspberry red. [All laugh]

In this extract the actual word 'jealous' is not mentioned but April certainly implies it. The twins' partners feel that the twins put each other first. The kind of jealousy described by April is similar to that mentioned by Norma in the previous extract; that is, the close relationship of twins becoming 'problematic' for others. April is aware that their partners did not want to occupy the 'second best' position but have come to accept that status – because it is unchangeable; the twins will always be first to each other.

Conclusion

The concept of a couple solves the problem of misunderstanding twins to some extent but creates another because twins are also quite different from couples. For example, romantic couples have generally not shared their childhood; they grow up in different environments and meet at some point later in life. Also, a romantic couple relationship may develop from a friendship that later becomes attraction. That is not the case with twin relationships. Twins develop together from the very onset of their lives. In addition, twins often experience identity confusion but no such obvious identity confusion exists with couples. Above all, members of a couple come together by choice, while identical twins do not choose to be a pair – they are born as such.

In spite of these differences, a couple, as we can see in the twins' own accounts, can be used as a metaphor for understanding twins in a social context like that of Western society, where representations of individual differences are dominant and where there is a strong resemblance between twins and romantic couples. Research suggests that many similarities exist between romantic couples and identical twins; for example, their bond, team approach, joint ownership, power relations, similarity, companionship, complementarity, interdependence and jealousy.

In the interviews I conducted, the twins positioned themselves as couples by using words that portray them as a unit, such as 'we', 'us' and 'our'. This was particularly the case in relation to the themes of bonding and joint identity. Not only does this make a connection between twins and couples but it also paints a picture that twins can use to help other people understand their identity. That is, other people can draw on the metaphor of a couple to understand twin identity.

When twins apply the couple metaphor to describe themselves, however, it may add to the problem of being misunderstood, particularly in Western societies that embrace individual differences.

The metaphor of couples was applied by the twins in different ways. For example, in Chapter 4 it emerged in the theme of joint identity. Norma stated:

> I am a twin … I don't know, my twin is a part of me; I can't change that and neither can she.

Here, Norma identifies herself not as an individual but as a member of a couple. She indicates their connection and what they mean to each other. Strong bonds and companionship are also elements of romantic couple relationships.

> The metaphor of the romantic couple also emerges when discussing the performance of twin identity.

It is important also to note that the twins in this study used the metaphor of couples to work against being seen as individuals As a consequence, individualisation, despite being so strongly represented in contemporary culture, becomes ambiguous here. The twins consistently stated, across many themes, that being associated with 'couples' works against individualism. The psychological notion that each person is a unique autonomous individual. (The accounts of accounts of twins indicate that the notion does not apply well for identical twins.)

Seymour-Smith and Wetherell (2006) asserted that bonds operate in romantic couple relationships and the identical twins in this study asserted that they too share a strong bond. The bond in twins was associated with love for one another, doing things together, talking to each other, mutuality of feelings and common interests. Bonds can be developed in the same way in romantic couples.

Seymour-Smith and Wetherell also assert that couples perform and manage their 'coupleness'. They observed that the couples who took part in their study worked hard to present a unified image of a positive, very close, harmonious relationship. Even though one partner in each couple had cancer, they talked about it as though it was a shared diagnosis, a form of 'joint authorship'. I noticed something similar during the interview process in my study – the identical twins also performed their 'twinness' (by completing each other's sentences, dressing similarly and using the rhetoric of couples to describe their relationship).

Butler (1988) suggested that uttering the phrase 'I love you' changes the dynamic in a romantic couple's relationship – it creates a situation of no return. Saying is doing, Butler states. The words people say to each other affect and have consequences for feelings, thoughts and actions. Social discourses about twins similarly affect how twins understand themselves and are understood by others. Butler goes on to say that romantic love is a social construction that does not exist before verbally expressed. It follows therefore that the understanding of romantic love that exists in couple relationships, like twin identity, cannot be separated from the socio-cultural context but can be looked at through the lens of historical perspective in order to see how it has evolved over time.

It is worth mentioning that the strong bonds and closeness that characterise twin relationships can potentially cause problems in romantic couple relationships if the partner to a twin fails to understand and appreciate the special relationship that exists between twin siblings. It is also possible that a twin sibling, who is very close and bonded with their twin may have to deal with 'separation stress' when committing to a romantic relationship, which may negatively affect the romantic relationship. In addition, to maintain their special bond while engaged in romantic relationships, twins might have to make compromises regarding the amount of time and attention they give to their romantic partner. This may cause their partner to feel like they are competing with the other twin for love and attention, leading to jealousy and, potentially, other problems too.

Research further shows that couples tend to team up in their functioning. Wetherell and Dixon (2004) reported that many couples engage in shared activities, which is also the case with twins, as their accounts demonstrated. They repeatedly stressed how much they enjoy doing things together. Another similarity between twins and romantic couples is joint ownership of assets. Wetherell and Dixon (2004) asserted that many couples spend their income collectively, which has the effect of strengthening their commitment to each other. Many of the identical twins in this study mentioned sharing 'everything', including their clothes. If twins feel that they share a joint identity, so too may couples – particularly if they choose to have the same surname.

Power imbalances are often discussed as an element of heterosexual romantic couple relationships; men often enjoy more privileges than women, sometimes at their expense (Maher and Singleton, 2013). Indeed, it has been argued that heterosexual romantic relationships obscure and disguise gender inequality and the oppression of women. Similar power relations may operate in identical twin relationships. In this study, twins referred to dominating or being dominated by the other twin; of feeling in control and controlled. The power imbalance within a twin relationship resembles the inequality often experienced by the female partner in a romantic couple.

Gendered discourse in a patriarchal society assigns different roles to men and women in relation to romantic love. Hollway (1989) identified what she called a 'have/hold' discourse that complements the 'male sex drive' and 'reproductive/nurturing' view of a heterosexual relationship. Indeed, this discourse can also be seen as gender insensitive because it implies that sex should occur only within a committed relationship, a 'rule' that, in practice, is applied more stringently to women than men. Hollway further argued that romantic love is a modern social construction, which tends to disempower women. I argue that the social and structural barriers that control women in romantic couple relationships also contribute to the way in which twin relationships are misunderstood.

In research into romantic relationships conducted by Kamla-Raj (2008), women stated that they expected the following from their partner: connectedness, mutual support, companionship, loyalty, commitment, physical and emotional intimacy and a higher kind of union. They suggested that being in a romantic relationship that involved these elements would increase their self-esteem. Such high expectations may make people very distressed when a relationship fails.

The bonds and interdependence highlighted in the accounts in this study indicate that twins are locked together in deeply intense psychological ways. This closeness can potentially cause twins to be extra demanding of their partners' time, energy and attention in romantic relationships because, from birth, they have received constant companionship from each other. This may contribute to the problem of being misunderstood by their partners. Another thing that appears to be misunderstood about twins, and that emerged in their accounts, is the level of loneliness that they experience when they are mature and have to commit to romantic relationships. The separation from their twin appears to leave them with a sense of pain and emptiness that is hard for other people to understand. If not supported properly, that hard phase of separation may leave twins with emotional and psychological scars. I suggest that more research be conducted into this issue in order to provide support for twins who are dealing with this separation anxiety at any stage of life. Preferably, such research, and support projects, should involve twins studying and helping other twins, because their accounts indicate that a 'twin world' and 'twin things' exist that non-twins will never understand.

In this chapter, I discussed the theme of jealousy in relation to twin relationships and highlighted that twins also experience distress when one leaves the twin relationship to commit to a romantic partner. I consider it a reasonable conclusion that, when close relationships like those of twins and romantic couples fail, those involved suffer severe emotional and psychological pain – particularly the 'other half' who is left behind. Those who end or change the relationship may experience a sense of guilt as a result of knowing how the rejected other is feeling. Jealousy appears to operate in both romantic couple and twin relationships, as the interviews in this study bore out.

The aim of this chapter was to show that a romantic couple can be used as a frame of reference for understanding twins in a social – Western – context that values individual difference. I highlighted that twins speak of themselves by drawing on couple relationships, using words that portray them as a unit. I suggest that this link between twins and couples can be used by twins to help others understand their identity.

I have established, through a variety of themes, the different ways in which twins draw on couple discourses when describing their lives. Although I have underlined the similarities between twins and couples, it needs to be noted that there are factors that are exclusive to twins and have nothing to do with couples, for example physical intimacy. Above all, couples come together through choice, while identical twins are simply born into a couple-like relationship. It is important, however, to note that twins' use of the couples metaphor may work against others understanding them within a culture based on individualism. The next chapter will outline findings of this book.

6
TWINS, CULTURE AND PSYCHOLOGY

In this chapter, I briefly outline my findings before describing the contributions this book makes to twin research, its practical implications and those who might benefit from it. I also discuss the limitations of my study and ideas for future research.

The connections between the relationships of twins and couples that were highlighted in the data and discussed within the frame of psychological literature pertaining to couples include: bonds (Seymour-Smith and Wetherell, 2006); joint ownership of assets (Wetherell and Dixon, 2004); power relations issues (Maher and Singleton, 2013); interdependence (Miller, 1976); companionship (Kalmijn, 2001); friendship (White, 1983); jealousy (Kalmijn, 2001); a team approach (Wetherell and Dixon 2004); performance (Seymour-Smith and Wetherell, 2006); and similarity of attitude toward life (Hill et al., 1976).

In relation to identity, I highlighted that, contrary to the abstract, ostensibly objective ways in which psychological research speaks about twin identity, a complex web of cultural and societal influences informs how twins construct and claim their identities. I also observed an interesting contradiction in the ways in which twins perceive themselves and speak about their identity: the majority of the twins interviewed in this study embraced and articulated joint identity and similarity; the minority criticised these aspects of twinship in favour of individual uniqueness.

Making use of Goffman's (1959) discursive framing of rhetorical constructions that takes and and analyses examples relating to various themes, I discussed how identical twins also become dramatic and theatrical performers of their identities. This performance took the form of dressing similarly to display themselves as 'typical twins'; they also spoke of impersonating each other, for fun or to achieve a particular outcome.

On a different note, I used the work of Butler (1997) to discuss how twin identity is a product of social construction. I highlighted how 'forces' operating within the social context of twins are active and influential in shaping their identity. This issue was addressed using the theme of similarity, and indeed twins spoke of being pressured to act in uniform ways. I discussed also how twin identity is described by some twins as 'something from within' and situated this finding in the light of Cattell (1966), who assumes that people do not act out or manage the impression they give to others; they have only one 'honest' identity. In such accounts, identity is synonymous with their disposition and they identify completely with it. In my study, twins repeatedly used phrases to emphasise their similarity in both appearance and nature. Their reference to being connected 'in the blood' relates both to the social construction of 'everyday' notions of identity and the lack of recognition they feel their specific twin relationship receives within that construction.

I have also demonstrated that twins' descriptions of be themselves differ from their representation in the psychological literature and popular culture. Here, I brought to light how the idea of individual differences can result in identical twins being misunderstood. They do not correspond to the notion of individualism that is taken for granted in Western society. From the opposite perspective, I have been able to show that individualism does not correspond with the experience of being a twin.

The analysis in Chapter 3 used, among other sources, the work of Gaillard et al. (2009), who suggested that Western cultures particularly value individual differences and personal uniqueness; people are taught to respect individual rights, embrace individual liberty and to reject norms and conformity. This chapter also used the work of Rose (1985) to highlight how the 'governmentalisation' of the individual fails to appreciate variables between subjects; that twins are individuals as well as twins is thus not recognised or understood.

The discussion also explored the possibly that, because twins are born as a pair and spend their childhood and young adulthood together, they have limited experience of life as individuals. Their desire to embrace a joint identity led to them being misunderstood, they felt. This point was illustrated using the theme of marital problems, where twins spoke of 'buying one and getting one for free'. Condon's (2008) ideas were also used in the discussion, particularly the 13 signs that suggest an individual might be feeling misunderstood, in order to discuss the different ways in which twins expressed this feeling.

This book has added to the body of existing work on twin identity in many ways, as the overarching meta-thematic analysis I have just presented demonstrates. It shows how twins talk about themselves and persistently takes apart hegemonic representations of 'subjects' in various ways. To start with, this book has shown how twins' representations of themselves and their relationships work continuously to undermine dominant representations of 'individual subjects', both directly, by setting twins and their own particular individuality against 'individuals', and less directly, by articulating themes around 'similarity' and 'the couple' that characterise twin's talk about themselves. In so doing, this study has, unlike mainstream psychological studies, attended to the voices of twins. It used an interview method that includes life story research and semi-structured, open-ended questions that gave twins sufficient freedom and space to express themselves fully, thus providing new insights that have not been studied before.

My research not only used a social constructionist approach in an area where no one has used it before but I also applied it in a unique way too. It is unique because I conducted the interviews after reviewing core psychological themes addressed in twin studies, and analysing some prevalent representations of twins in popular culture. This embedded the interviews in a cultural context in a very explicit way, thus taking seriously, in the operationalisation of my research, the notion of cultural construction from the very beginning. I further used the understanding gained from these cultural representations to help me interpret the accounts gathered from the interviews. Social constructionist studies tend to assume they know the characteristics of a particular cultural context; my research makes the case for a thorough and specific investigation of cultural context to guide the research. Many social constructionist studies focus only on cultural representations, or only on how people speak about their identity; this book has done both. Moreover, using a social constructionist approach has helped me show how social constructions co-exist, with people acting to reframe themselves, resisting certain constructions and dominant discourses.

As a result of all of the above, the book has provided an alternative perspective on understanding twin identity, one that mainstream psychological studies do not provide because the use traditional research methods. Burr (2003, p. 149) puts it this way: 'We cannot investigate the psychological and social world by using our old practices and assumptions.'

My work has taken up the contributions but also the limitations of mainstream psychology, particularly in terms of how its ideas appear in popular culture and in twins' accounts. I have highlighted twin voices and shown some aspects of twinship that have not been revealed before; for example, their sense of being misunderstood, the idea of misunderstanding oneself, and the links made between twins and the metaphor of a couple. I have also shown that twin identity does not fit with Western representations of individuals. Twin identity has, of course, been addressed before, but this book is unique in that it has explored the subject from the perspective of twins from different socio-economic backgrounds and locations and of different age, gender and ethnicity, including both immigrant and non-immigrant pairs.

I have also shown how the notion of individualism joins the three aspects of twin identity, namely: the metaphor of a couple, the theme of being misunderstood and the different dimensions of twin identity. Overall, my detailed investigation of twin identity using semi-structured, life narrative interviews and thematic analysis has brought to light the multi-layered complexity of twin identity.

Other than showing that particular themes are constantly found in different media at different times, this book has provided a socio-cultural analytic context for researchers interested in looking at twins' identity or at accounts of twins' lives. I have used the twins' narratives to demonstrate the link between twin relationships, their identity and the metaphor of a romantic couple. The book has further highlighted that using this metaphor could help twins deal with issues of individuality and with being treated as a unit. No other twin study has brought this issue to light.

I have also demonstrated how the couple metaphor can be used to solve the dual problem of others misunderstanding twins and twins struggling to understand themselves. (I did bear in mind, however, that drawing on the concept of couples can create other problems because twins are not exactly like them.) This is another novel contribution, which no other study has highlighted. By citing research on couples and linking it to the personal accounts of twins, I have shown that the metaphor of couples can be used as a frame of reference for understanding twins in a social context, Western societies, where notions of individual difference are dominant.

Another finding which this book has contributed to the body of knowledge on twins concerns the way in which they are misunderstood. I have shown that when twins function as a pair in a culture dominated by individual differences, such as the one in which this study was conducted, there are problems which can be solved by looking at twin identity and relationships using the metaphor of a couple.

I have also brought to light the way in which the notion of individual difference causes a problem in terms of being misunderstood for identical twins, showing that, by virtue of being identical twins, they do not seem to fully correspond with the notion of individualism that is taken for granted in Western society. They do not identify with or fit into it because twins in a way *are* a couple. I demonstrated this point by revealing twins' accounts of taking advantage of their similarity by swapping roles to deceive others; these actions suggesting that they do not perceive themselves as individuals but as similar. This can create a problem for those around them who might view that twin behaviour in light of their own, Western, socio-cultural context. This book has shown that twins further complicate the puzzle of their identity through their avoidance of singular personal pronouns when speaking of themselves, which indirectly implies a joint identity, in a culture where people are mostly treated as individuals.

Furthermore, in this book I have brought to light the dynamics of twin identity, particularly the ways in which it is constructed and performed by identical twins in different ways in accordance with their social setting and audience. I have also demonstrated that the twins' identity in this research was performed to an imagined audience, and that there is no uniformity in the way twins construct and claim their identity. I was able to demonstrate that there are contradictions in how twins speak of themselves, and in how they construct and claim their identities. I provided examples of interviewees either claiming a special twin identity or, in direct contrast, describing themselves as ordinary and no different from non-twins.

I conducted my research according to theme, which allowed me to make associations between them to provide a fuller picture of twin experience. For example, on the theme of identity confusion I used data gathered on the theme of similarity to show that such confusion often results from parents treating twins as a unit.

This book has further brought to light something else that no other research has identified: the complexity of twin identity and twins' misunderstanding of themselves. I revealed that this misunderstanding results from both their upbringing and how they are treated as a unit in society. Another way in which this book has contributed to the body of knowledge on twins concerns its underlining of the different dimensions that contribute to how they are misunderstood. The dimensions emerged in a thematic format and included strange knowledge, blame, marital problems and identity confusion.

Directions for future research

One of the motives of this study was to open a window into twin identity and thus I will now present my recommendations for future research. I have already discussed a potential area for further investigation, which has to do with the implications of the social representations of and discourses about twins. As I argued earlier, mainstream psychological studies on twins appear to have ignored the consequences of the discourses they have helped to create about them; no study seems to have investigated the impact of these discourses and so future research could follow up on this.

In Chapter 1, I presented an analysis of cultural representations in a selection of texts (films, books and plays) and mentioned that they covered the period from the early sixteenth century to the twenty-first century. They thus range from the time of William Shakespeare to modern-day films and books. Here, I had neither the time nor space to consider how these representations have changed over time. Other studies might specifically look at changes in cultural representations of twins over the centuries and at the specific ways in which identical twins are viewed in different genres of film, play and book. I would expect these fictional representations to be different in documentaries, where identical twins actually produce some of the text by speaking for themselves.

Another potentially interesting area of research is to analyse the different ways in which male and female identical twins are represented. Other studies could follow up on that issue.

I expect that twin representations in Western culture are different to those found in other areas of the world, especially those that traditionally focus on the spoken word and less importance is afforded to films and novels. Other studies could thus examine cultures that rely on a verbal tradition to investigate whether twin representations are different in those contexts and, if so, in what ways. I could also have presented in a chrono-logical manner the different fictional representations that I analysed in Chapter 1; however, I wanted to show how specific themes run across different texts. A narrative study could thus be carried out to reflect the chronology more precisely.

Having shown in this study some of the ways in which psychology influences culture, for example in terms of how twins use psychological ideas in their accounts, it would be interesting for future research to also look at how psychological ideas form part of these cultural representations and how psychological theories feed into popular culture.

Another issue, which is the flip-side of this same point, is that future studies could look at the influence of cultural representations on psychological research, and particularly at the way in which psychological research takes ideas from cultural representations in order to develop theories. There could be a possible argument that these theories too are socially constructed. I have shown elements of this in my analysis of popular cultural representations and in the way in which twins have spoken to me, making reference to psycho-logical theories. Future studies can build on my work in this respect.

Furthermore, other thematic issues could enhance further understanding of twin identity, such as gender difference, ethnicity and age. These factors seemed central in the twins' accounts in this study. Age, for example, was shown to be a significant issue in twin identity at various stages but demographic factors appear to have little influence. What matters is what is in their blood. It is important to mention that mainstream psychological studies, using quantitative approaches, have taken some of those factors into account but no one has done so with twin experiences and through use of a qualitative approach. Future studies could investigate this claim further by exploring the impact of demographic factors on sets of twins that were brought up in different environments.

Family is mentioned a great deal in the twins' accounts, in relation to all of the themes I raised. This suggests that the notion of family plays a key role in different aspects of twin identity, and future studies could thus focus more closely on how it influences the development of such.

Since this study considered twin identity from a British multi-ethnic perspective, it is my suggestion that a richer and more comprehensive understanding of twin identity could focus on the accounts of twins located within and between ethnicities. Further studies could investigate why twins speak differently about their identity according to their ethnicity. It is indeed noteworthy that the black and Filipino participants in this study did not claim to have a special twin identity, unlike the white participants; in fact, they described themselves as 'normal people'. This too can be further investigated by conducting a between-groups study focusing on the accounts of identity provided by black twins and white twins.

As this study explored themes across many transcripts, it would be ideal for other studies to use a case study approach to consider the individual biography of each set of twins. This more in-depth analysis would produce a comprehensive understanding of each transcript in terms of twin identity and other aspects of twins' lives. An in-depth analysis such as this could also return to the interviews and analyse the way in which twins gave their accounts to me, as a particular type of researcher. For example, one set of twins from Bradford raised the issue of race and made angry comments about immigration, which I did not have space to explore in detail in this study. I merely highlighted the issue, but other studies could follow up on it.

I have argued that a qualitative – and, more specifically, a social constructionist approach – would be the most suitable for studying and analysing the twins' accounts. I discussed the fact that this approach throws the whole approach of mainstream psychology into question. I argue that more critical and qualitative approaches should be used to study twins' accounts. Especially suitable would be those approaches that go beyond language, because the meaning of what is said can be found between the lines too; for example, by looking at implicit ideas or by focusing on what is communicated through laughter, stammering, gestures and hesitations.

REFERENCES

Andrews, F. M. and Withey, S. B. (1976). *Social indicators of well-being*. New York: Doubleday.

Appiah, A. (2014). Race, culture, identity: Misunderstood connections. *Social Theory and Practice: Race and Racism*, 24, 92–101.

Argyle, M. (2009). *The psychology of happiness*, 2nd edition. New York: Routledge.

Aries, P. (1962). *Centuries of childhood: A social history of family life*. New York: Vintage.

Arther, B. (1997). *Faces of degeneration: A European disorder*. Cambridge: Cambridge University Press.

Bass, K. (Dir.) (1982). *Sister, Sister*. Birmingham, AL: Fox Television.

Baxter, H. (2014). *Prenatal risk factors*. New York: Doubleday.

Berger, P. and Luckmann, T. (eds) (1991). *The social construction of reality: A treatise in the sociology of knowledge*. New York: Doubleday.

Bernardes, J. (1997). *Family studies: An introduction*. London: Routledge.

Bible, The (1978). *New King James version*. Nashville, TN: Thomas Nelson Inc.

Billig, M. (1978). *Fascists: A social psychological view of the National Front*. New York: Harcourt Brace.

Billig, M. (2014). Undiscipled beginnings, academic success, and discursive psychology. *British Journal of Social Psychology*, 51, 413–424.

Blood, R. O. and Wolfe, D. M. (1960). *Husbands and wives: The dynamics of married living*. New York: Free Press.

Bordwell, D. and Thompson, K. (1997). *Film art: An introduction*. New York: McGraw-Hill.

Bouchard, T. J. (1994). Genes, environment and personality. *Science*, 26, 170–177.

Bouchard, T. J. (1995). Breaking the last taboo. *Contemporary Psychology*. New York: Cambridge University Press.

Brady, N. R. (2004). A portrait of families with a member labelled schizophrenic. *Journal of Rogerian Nursing Science*, 42, 311–321.

Branagh, K. (Dir.) (2013). *The Comedy of Errors*. www.youtube.com/watch?v= 6i3J17JpOag [Accessed 12 February 2014].

Brannen, J., Moss, P. and Mooney, A. (2004). *Working and caring over the twentieth century: Change and continuity in four-generation families*. ESRC Future of Work Series. Basingstoke: Palgrave Macmillan.

Braun, V. and Clarke, V. (2006). Using thematic analysis in psychology. *Qualitative Research in Psychology*, 3, 77–101.

Brent, R. W. (2000). The rank-order consistence of personality traits from childhood to old age. *Qualitative Review of Longitudinal Studies*, 1, 3–25.

Burr, V. (2003). *Social constructionism*. London: Routledge.

Burr, V. (2015). *Social constructionism*, 3rd edition. London: Routledge.

Burt, C. L. (1917). *The distribution and relations of educational abilities*. London: Campfield Press.

Burt, S. A. (2009). Rethinking environmental contributions to child and adolescent psychopathology: A meta-analysis of shared environmental influences. *Psychology Bulletin*, 35, 608–637.

Burtt, C. (1972). Inheritance of general intelligence. *American Psychologist*, 27, 175–190.

Butler, J. (1988). Performative acts and gender constitution: An essay in phenomenology and feminist theory. *Theatre Journal*, 40(4), 519–531.

Butler, J. (1997). *Excitable speech: A politics of the performative*. New York: Routledge.

Cabell, C. (2002). *The Kray brothers: The image shattered*. London: Robson Books.

Cattell, R. B. (1966). *The scientific analysis of personality*. Chicago, IL: Aldine.

Chatman, S. (1990). *Story and discourse: Narrative structure in fiction and film*. Ithaca, NY: Cornell University Press.

Chatwin, B. (1996). *On the black Hill*. London: Pan Books.

Condon, B. B. (2008). Feeling misunderstood: A concept analysis. *Journal of Counselling Psychology*, 4, 177–190.

Coppel, A. (1967). *Tweedledum and Tweedledee*. London: Geoffrey Bles.

Cronenberg, D. (Dir.) (1988). *Dead ringers*. Toronto: Revok Films.

Culpepper, H. M. (Dir.) (2011). *Deadly sibling rivalry*. Los Angeles, CA: Maple Island Films.

Davis, E. A. (1937). *Linguistic skills in twins, singletons with siblings and only children from age five to ten years*. Minnesota: University of Minnesota Press.

Davis, M., Bolding, G., Hart, G., Sheer, L. and Elford, J. (2004). Reflecting on the experience of interviewing online: Perspectives from the Internet and HIV study in London. *AIDS Care*, 8, 944–952.

Day, E. (1932). The development of language in twins: A comparison of twins and single children. *Child Development*, 3, 179–99.

Deng, A. et al. (2016). Ancestry variation and footprints of natural selection along the genome in Latin American populations. *Scientific Reports*, 6. doi: 10.1038/srep21766.

Duru, G., Auray, J. P., Gaudin, A. F., Dartigues, J. F., Henry, P. and Lanteri-Minet, M. (2004). Impact of headache on quality of life in a general population survey in France. *Headache: The Journal of Head and Face Pain*, 44, 571–580.

Eaves, L. J. (1972). *Twins as a basis for the causal analysis of human personality*. New York: Doubleday.

Edwards, R. (2002). *Mature women students: Separating or connecting family and education*. London: Taylor & Francis.

Farah, M. (2013). I missed my twin brother Hassan so much during our 12-year separation. *Daily Telegraph*, 6 October. www.telegraph.co.uk/sport/othersports/athletics/10359526/Mo-Farah-I-missed-my-twin-brother-Hassan-so-much-during-our-12-year-separation.html [Accessed 1 July 2015].

Farber, S. L. (1981). *Identical twins reared apart*. New York: Basic Books.

Fahy, E. (2010). Facts about twins. http.ohbaby.co.nz/baby/twins [Accessed 1 March 2012].

Festinger, L. (1954). A theory of social comparison process. *Human Relations*, 117–140.

Fleishman, A. (1992). *Narrated films: Storytelling situations in cinema history*. Baltimore, MD: Johns Hopkins University Press.

Fox, D. and Prilletensky, I. (1997). *Critical psychology: An introduction*. London: Sage.

Gaillard, S. Mosey, L. and Thomas, P. S. (2009). Mental health patients' experiences of being misunderstood. *Journal of the American Psychiatric Nurses Association*, 15, 191–199.

Gale, T. (2006). Twin studies: Research article from *World of Genetics*. www.bookrags.com/research/twin-studies-wog [Accessed 7 January 2012].

Galton, F. (1874). *English men of science: Their nature and nurture*. London: Frank Press.

Gedda, L. (1961). *Twins in history and in science*. Springfield, IL: Charles Thomas Press.

Gerler, J. (1991). Perspectives on human communication research: Behaviourism, phenomenology, and an integrated view. *Western Journal of Speech Communication*, 48, 277–292.

Gillies, V. (2003). *Pulling together, pulling apart: The family lives of young people*. London: Rowntree Foundation.

Gillies, V., Ribbens McCarthy, J. and Holland, J. (2001). *Pulling together, pulling apart: The family lives of young people*. London: Rowntree Foundation.

Goffman, E. (1959). *The presentation of self in everyday life*. New York: Doubleday.

Goffman, E. (1968). *Stigma: Notes on the management of spoiled identity*. New York: Penguin.

Gottschall, J. (2012). *Why fiction is good for you*. www.bostonglobe.com/ideas/2012/04/28/why-fiction-good-for-youhowfictionchanges-your-world/nubDy1P3viDj2PuwGwb3KO/story.html [Accessed 8 August 2012].

Griffin, C. (2000). *More than simply talk and text: Psychologist as cultural ethnographers*. London: Routledge.

Hall, S. (1997). *Representation: Cultural representations and signifying practices*. London: Sage.

Harré, R. and Secord, P. F. (1972). *The explanation of social behaviour*. Oxford: Blackwell.

Harré, R. and Langenhove, L. van (1998). *Positioning theory: Moral contexts of intentional action*. Oxford: Blackwell.

Henderson, D. K. and Gillespie, R. D. (1927). *A textbook of psychiatry for student an practitioners*. Oxford: Oxford University Press.

Henelotter, F. (Dir.) (1982). *Basket Case*. New York: Tartan Video.

Henelotter, F. (Dir.) (1990). *Basket Case 2*. New York: Synapse Films.

Henriques, J., Hollway, W., Urwin, C., Venn, C. and Walkerdine, V. (1984). *Changing the subject: Psychology, social regulation and subjectivity*. London: Methuen.

Hill, C. T., Rubin, A. and Peplau, L. A. (1976). Breakups before marriage: The end of 103 affairs. *Journal of Social Issues*, 32, 147–168.

Hollway, D. (1989). *Subjectivity and method in psychology*. London: Sage.

Holzinger, K. J. (1892). *An experimental book of inheritance*. Chicago, IL: University of Chicago Press.

Hsu, F. L. K. (1948). *Under the ancestors' shadow: Chinese culture and personality*. New York: Columbia University Press.

Hunter, T. (Dir.) (1991). *Lies of the twins*. Chicago, IL: Universal Studios.

Jeffereys, K. (1994). R.A. Butler, the Board of Education and the 1944 Education Act. *History*, 69, 415–431.

Jonas-Simpson, C. M. (2001). Feeling understood: A melody of human becoming. *Nursing Science Quarterly*, 14, 222–230.

Jose, R. (1991). *The founders of humanistic psychology*. Westport, CT: Praeger.

Joseph, C. (2004). *The gene illusion: Genetic research in psychiatry and psychology under the microscope*. New York: Algora Publishing.

Joseph, E. D. and Tabor, J. H. (1961). The simultaneous analysis of a pair of identical twins and the twinning reaction. *Psychoanalytic Study of the Child*, 16, 275–299.

Joseph, J. (2015). *The trouble with twin studies: A reassessment of twin research in the social and behavioural sciences*. London: Routledge.

Juel-Nielsen, N. (1980). *Individual and environment: Monozygotic twins reared apart*, revised edition. New York: International Universities Press.

Kalmijn, M. (2001). Joint and separated lifestyles in couple relationships. *Journal of Marriage and Family*, 3, 639–654.

Kamin, L. (1974). *The science and politics of I. Q.* New York: Wiley.

Kamla-Raj, G. (2008). Romantic love in heterosexual relationships: Women's experiences. *Journal of Social Sciences*, 3, 187–197.

Karin (2011). Heritability of Parkinson's disease in Swedish twins: A longitudinal study. *Neurological Disorders and Brain Damage*, 32, 1–8.

Kim, H. and Markus, H. R. (1999). Deviance or uniqueness, harmony or conformity? A cultural analysis. *Journal of Personality and Social Psychology*, 4, 785–800.

Kitzinger, C. (2008). Developing feminist conversation analysis: A response to Wowk. *Feminism and Psychology*, 10, 163–193.

Klamin, U. and Goldberger, K. D. (2000). Increased occurrence of schizophrenia and other psychiatric illnesses among twins. *British Journal of Psychiatry*, 168, 688–692.

Lassers, E. and Nordan, R. (1978). Separation–individuation of an identical twin. *Adolescent Psychiatry*, 6, 469–479.

Lather, P. (2009). Against empathy, voice and authenticity. In A. Y. Jackson and L. A. Mazzei (eds), *Voice in qualitative inquiry: Challenging conventional, interpretive, and critical conceptions in qualitative research* (pp. 17–26). London: Routledge.

Lothe, J. (2000). *Narrative in fiction and film: An introduction*. Oxford: Oxford University Press.

Lykken, D. T. (1982). EEG spectra in twins: Evidence for a neglected mechanism of genetic determination. *Physiological Psychology*, 10, 60–65.

Lykken, D. T. and Tellegen, A. (1996). Happiness is a stochastic phenomenon. *Psychological Science*, 7, 186–189.

Lykken, D. T., Bouchard, T. J., Tellegen, A. and McGue, M. (1993). Is human mating adventurous or the result of lawful choice? A twin study of mate selection. *Journal of Personality and Social Psychology*, 65, 56–68.

Maher, J. and Singleton, A. (2013). 'I wonder what he's saying': Investigating domestic discourse in young cohabitating heterosexual couples. *Journal of Marriage*, 21, 59–77.

Martin, C. (2011). *Twin studies*. London: Sage.

Miller, B. C. (1976). A multivariate developmental model of marital satisfaction. *Journal of Marriage and the Family*, 38, 643–657.

Mitchell, J. (1971). *Women's estate*. Harmondsworth: Penguin.

Mittler, P. (1970). *The study of twins*. Harmondsworth: Penguin.

Morris, V. (1997). Family involvement in education: The role of teacher education. Paper presented at the Annual Meeting of the American Educational Research Association, Chicago, IL.

Moscovici, S. (2001). Ideas and their development: A dialogue between Serge Moscovici and Ivana Markov. In S. Moscovici, *Social representations: Explorations in social psychology*. New York: New York University Press.

Mottet, E. (1999). Heterosexual couples talking about and doing gender. *Sociology*, 37, 413–431.

Mount, M. (2007). Gentlemen of the bar. www.theguardian.com/lifeandstyle/2007/apr/10/fashion.features11 [Accessed 1 July 2015].

Murray, M. (2002). Connecting narrative and social representation theory in health research. *Social Science Information*, 4, 653–673.

Nadesan, M. H. (2008). *Governmentality, biopower, and everyday life*. New York: Doubleday.

Newman, H. H., Freeman, F. N. and Holzinger, K. J. (1937). *Twins: A study of heredity and environment*. Chicago, IL: University of Chicago Press.

Oxford English Dictionary (1933). Oxford: Oxford University Press.

Parker, I. (2007). *Qualitative psychology*. Buckingham: Open University Press.

Piaget, J. (1926). *Language and thought of the child*. London: Routledge.

Potter, J. (2012). Discourse analysis and discursive psychology. In H. Cooper (ed.), *APA handbook of research methods in psychology*. Vol. 2. *Quantitative, qualitative, neuropsychological and biological* (pp. 111–130). Washington, DC: American Psychological Association Press.

Potter, J. and Billig, M. (1992). Re-representing representations: Discussion of Raty and Snellman. *Chapters on Social Representations*, 1, 15–20.

Potter, J. and Wetherell, M. (1987). *Discourse and social psychology: Beyond attitudes and behaviour*. London: Sage.

Preedy, P. (2007). Meeting the educational needs of pre-school and primary aged twins and higher multiples. In A. C. Sandbank (ed.), *Twin and triplet psychology: A professional guide to working with multiples*. London: Routledge.

Puhl, J. (2011). Jaroslow Kacynski loses his political compass. www.spiegel.de/international/Europe [Accessed 13 March 2012].

Reader, K. and Edwards, R. (2001). *The Papin sisters*. Oxford: Oxford University Press.

Ribbens, J. (1994). *Mothers and their children: A feminist sociology of childrearing*. London: Sage.

Rogers, C. (1961). *On becoming a person*. Boston, MA: Houghton Mifflin.

Rose, N. (1985). *The psychological complex: Psychology, politics and society in England, 1869–1939.* London: Routledge.

Roseneil, S. (2006). On not living with a partner: Unpicking coupledom and cohabitation. *Sociological Research Online,* 3, 3–11.

Rossetti, Z., Arndt, K., Ashby, C., Chadwick, M. and Kasahara, M. (2008). I like others to not try to fix me: Recognizing and supporting the agency of individuals with developmental disabilities. *Intellectual and Developmental Disabilities,* 46, 364–375.

Rowe, D. C. (1983). Biometrical genetic models of self-reported delinquent behaviour: A twin study. *Behavioural Genetics,* 13, 473–489.

Rushdie, S. (1992). *Imaginary homelands.* Harmondsworth: Penguin.

Scott, J. W. (1991). The evidence of experience. *Critical Enquiry,* 4, 773–797.

Segal, N. (2010). Even bigger loss for twin of late Polish president. www.aolnews.com/2010/04/12/even-bigger-loss-for-twin-of-late-polishpresident [Accessed 13 March 2012].

Sereceno, R. (2004). *Social services in international perspective.* New Brunswick, NJ: Transaction Books.

Seymour-Smith, S. and Wetherell, M. (2006). 'What he hasn't told you': Investigating the micropolitics of gendered support in heterosexual couples' co-constructed accounts of illnesses. *Journal of Feminism and Psychology,* 1, 105–127.

Shields, J. (1962). *Monozygotic twins brought up apart and brought up together.* London: Oxford University Press.

Siemon, M. (1980). The separation–individuation process in adult twins. *American Journal of Psychotherapy,* 34, 387–400.

Skabelund, J. (2005). 'I just work here': Creating a front line that improves your bottom line. *America's Health Care Financial Managers,* 20, 7–10.

Stewart, E. (2000). *Exploring twins: Towards a social analysis of twins.* London: Palgrave Macmillan.

Swift, D. (Dir) (1961). *The Parent Trap.* Hollywood, CA: Walt Disney Studios.

Tomura, M. (2009). A prostitute's lived experiences of stigma. *Journal of Phenomenological Psychology,* 40, 51–84.

Tournier, M. ([1975] 1981). *Gemini.* Garden City, NY: Doubleday.

Trilling, L. (1974). *Sincerity and authenticity.* Cambridge, MA: Harvard University Press.

Ussher, J. M., Hunter, M., Browne, J. and Good, C. (2000). *Bad or dangerous to know? Representations of femininity in narrative accounts.* London: Routledge.

Voelklein, C. and Howarth, A. (2005). *Objectifying the researcher's representations: The use of pictures in social representations research.* London: Palgrave Macmillan.

Walker, L. O. and Avant, K. C. (2005). Strategies for theory construction in nursing. *Journal of Health Studies,* 13, 63–84.

Wallace, M. (1986). *The silent twins.* London: Simon & Schuster.

Walters, D. (1989). Heredity and crime: Bad genes or bad research? *Criminology,* 27, 455–585.

Wetherell, M. and Dixon, J. (2004). On discourse and dirty nappies: Gender, the division of household labour and the social psychology of distributive justice. *Theory and Psychology,* 2, 167–189.

White, L. K. (1983). Determinants of spousal interaction: Marital structure or marital happiness. *Journal of Marriage and the Family*, 45, 511–519.

White, P. (1966). *The solid mandala*. London: Northumberland Press.

Wikipedia (n.d.). June and Jennifer Gibbons. en.wikipedia.org/wiki/June_and_Jennifer_Gibbons [Accessed 6 August 2012].

INDEX